ELUCIDATIONS

Light on Christian controversies

John Twisleton

Copyright © 2021 John Twisleton

All rights reserved.

Unless otherwise stated, scripture quotations are taken from the New Revised Standard Version of the Bible, Anglicised edition, copyright © 1989, 1995 by the Division of Christian Education of the National Council of the Churches of Christ in the United States of America.

Every effort has been made to research copyright owners for material used in this resource. The author apologies for any inadvertent omissions or errors, and would ask those concerned to contact him so that full acknowledgment or corrections can be made in the future.

No part of this book may be reproduced, or stored in a retrieval system, or transmitted in any form or by any means, electronic, mechanical, photocopying, recording, or otherwise, without express written permission of the publisher

ISBN: 9798718788198

Commendations

"Elucidations" means, of course, making lucid, shining light on something and here Dr Twisleton illumines a diversity of issues that can often become clouded. Elucidations is a mind-opening, spirit-expanding book that revisits significant questions of our time, distilling wisdom gained from over 40 years of ministry in contexts as diverse as South America and Sussex. This is a self-confessed "risky book" for courageously it does not shy away from painful issues. It does not necessarily invite agreement but rather engagement, stimulating us to re-think. It is hopeful, honest and challenging, springing from John's personal experience, forged in the interplay between Christian tradition and contemporary thinking. and enriched by insights from Anglican, Catholic, Orthodox and Reformed traditions.

Andrew D. Mayes, writer and associate professor, St George's College Jerusalem

These concise essays (addressing topics currently sometimes discussed with more heat than light, and sometimes nervously avoided) encourage exploration, inviting the enquirer who wonders whether Christianity is reasonable at all, and also the Christian reader seeking to clarify or explain its apparently counter-cultural aspects. Reason and faith – grounded in the author's decades of personal and pastoral experience, incorporating reflection on Scripture and tradition – are here brought to bear on a range of questions, with the positive conviction that "elucidating God is a calling forth with the light of reason and the light of faith which together lift us beyond ourselves..."

Eleanor Relle

Would you like to chat with someone who knows God? Who really knows him, not just ideas about him? Then read this book. It's a short set of conversations on some really important topics and on every page there is wisdom. Evolution, Confession, Suffering, Loving Yourself, Guilt, Hell and the perspectives of God in other Faith traditions are just some of the subjects explored. Father John Twisleton is a gentle and kind teacher who welcomes you to think. I recommend you read this book and begin a conversation. It could change your life.

Peter Kerridge, Chief Executive of Premier Radio

As well as conducting oneself in society, the outer world, Christianity involves people undertaking an inner journey to clarify their sacred aims and ambitions, to decide which values and priorities to adopt. In this brave book, the Reverend John asks himself many deeply personal questions and addresses them with commendable honesty and humility. In a secular, materialist global culture, people might ask, "Why bother?" The reason being that such questions - about sin, belief in God, sexual politics, or 'right to life' issues, for example - cannot be solved by intellect alone, and do not go away. To live a truly meaningful life and make a genuine contribution to the well-being of society, whether you are Christian or not, this type of question must be faced and workable solutions found. This knowledgeable, bible specialist's revealing 'Elucidations' offer an insightful approach that will help and inspire many on life's challenging journey towards spiritual maturity and wisdom.

Larry Culliford, author of 'The Psychology of Spirituality', and, 'Much Ado About Something: A Vision of Christian Maturity' (www.LDC52.co.uk)

JOHN TWISLETON

Foreword by the Bishop of Lewes

In the social media age that we live in it is easy to assume that everyone who is sensible thinks the same way as we do. I have a passion for 1970s Classic Alfa Romeos and belong to a social media group comprising of people who also like 1970s Alfa Romeos. We agree in our self-made silo that these classic cars are wonderful, and if anyone from outside the group suggests that they are highly strung and prone to rust we seek to ridicule their position, even if we know there is an element of truth in what they suggest. However, even within the group there are questions that are never asked because they are too divisive such as 'What is the prettiest 1970s Alfa?' We do not answer or even discuss the evidence, rather we form smaller groups for people with shared viewpoints.

As a Church, we can suffer from the same characteristics. We are not always good at exploring the full depth of church teaching on issues that are relevant to our world today. John Twisleton challenges us to step out from our often well intentioned and precious silos and briefly explore some different perspectives. In doing so he does not necessarily wish us to change our own views, but to broaden our knowledge and understanding of those who might hold different views from our own, individuals who are also made in the image of God. The wide range of subjects briefly explored will help us to engage more fully with fellow Christians that we might more generously discuss controversial issues of faith. Elucidations will I believe also help us speak with confidence on a wide range of divisive areas with those who are exploring what faith might mean to them in the light of the pandemic.

+William Lewes

The Right Revd Will Hazlewood

JOHN TWISLETON

Contents

	Commendations	2
	Foreword	5
	Introduction	9
1	Anti-Semitic	13
2	Being Pro-Life	17
3	Believing in the Bible	21
4	Confession to a priest	25
5	Eco-friendly?	29
6	Elucidating God	35
7	Eucharistic controversy	39
8	Evolution and the Bible	43
9	Experience of the Holy Spirit	47
10	Gay Christians	51
11	God and the Cross	57
12	Guilt	61
13	Hell	65
14	Judgement	69
15	Loving yourself	73

16	Marian controversy	77
17	Ordination of women	83
18	Reasonable faith	87
19	Sin	91
20	So many denominations	95
21	So many faiths	101
22	Suffering	105
23	The Empty Tomb	109
24	Trusting the Church	113
25	Unanswered prayer	119
	Notes	123
	About the author	127
	Books by the author	128

Introduction

Each of the following essays invites the reader to gain light upon a controversial aspect of Christianity. These range from self-love to unanswered prayer, Mary to anti-Semitism, suffering to same sex unions, charismatic experience to the ordination of women, hell to ecology and trusting the Church, a total of twenty five essays. The elucidations are assembled without system save alphabetical order of title. The topics have got me thinking and learning over the years. My aim has been to provide distillations serving my readers and encouraging loyalty to the cause I believe will outlast us all.

'Elucidations' honours the 50th anniversary of the first edition of Hans Urs von Balthasar's Elucidations that dealt succinctly with questions for Christians that are either avoided or forgotten. In 1971 the author wrote: 'Certain problems today are given excessive publicity; men try to exalt them by force into 'articles by which the Church stands or falls'. They are practically all problems which men try to solve by smoothing over or playing down the difficulties, by suggesting, supposedly out of sympathy for men's needs, the easier way. And yet in the long run it is the narrow way which attracts the best men. It is, for example, well known that monasteries which have preserved the strictness of their disciplines undiminished today still have new postulants, whereas those who prefer a softer line seem to be despised by God and men. That is only intended to be taken as a symptom. The one who makes demands (but he must also give evidence that he has much to offer and must only make his demands for God and his work) still has a chance of being heard. It is part of the definition of fashion that it will change next year. That which is truly Christian was fortunately never fashionable, not even in the so-called Christian ages'.

Though an Anglican I warmed to the intriguing fashion-challenging thinking of this Roman Catholic writer distilling from the Christianity of his day a series of challenging lines. Over the last fifty years RC and Anglican traditions have developed in parallel impacted by movements both of renewal and adjustment to external challenges such as the environmental crisis. The Pentecostal movement addressed in my essays has meanwhile brought church growth away from the historic institutions of the church. Christianity in the west is now yet more unfashionable and church membership more decided. This decidedness is linked alas to a rise in fundamentalism of the unthinking kind addressed in my elucidations on reasonable faith as well as evolution and the bible. Decided membership is also linked to the seeming necessity of religious experience, despite warnings from scripture and Christian tradition that faith centres on God not self. As an Anglocatholic, who passed through a humiliating faith crisis enlarging God before me, I elucidate here what it means to give critical loyalty to scripture and tradition in the spirit of Balthasar. Like him I appreciate how doctrine, worship, ethics and prayer come together into the seamless 'whole' of catholic faith which, to me as an Anglican, is Christian faith in its fullness (Greek: καθολικός whole or full).

The demands of Christianity are rooted in doctrine as we try to live in the truth, especially that of baptism which puts paid to our sinful nature and helps us experience the Holy Spirit. In the essay on judgement I reflect on truth telling and how, just as we cannot live without clean water, we cannot function without clean information. 'Elucidations' is about clearing misconceptions of the truth that is in Jesus, the authority of the Bible and the trustworthiness of the Church. It is a risky book with essays on anti-Semitism, gay Christians and the ordination of women that attempt to balance love with truth and empathy with detachment from fashion. For any failings of perception here I apologise in advance. The Christian instinct to get alongside those at the sharp end of things is further addressed in an autobiographical elucidation of what it means to be 'pro-life' be that life in the womb, afflicted by injustice or vulnerable through old age. Again experience of the Holy Spirit is allied to that pro-life banner as Jesus taught: 'The Spirit of the Lord is upon me, because he has anointed me to bring good news to the poor. He has sent me to proclaim release to the captives and recovery of sight to the blind, to let the oppressed go free... I came that they may have life, and have it abundantly' (Luke 4:18 cf Isaiah 61:1, John 10:10b).

Whilst reasoned defence of Christianity in the 21st century still centres on the significance of Christ's death and resurrection awareness of other faiths has increased over the last fifty years due to enhanced communications. With so many faiths to choose from, people get confused. This book elucidates Christian faith in a context necessitating critical evaluation of world religions. In holding together God's closeness yet otherness Christianity is presented as the middle of a spectrum ranging from the transcendent vision of God in Islam to the more immanent vision of the divine found in Hindu society. Saying 'yes' to Jesus does not mean saying 'no' to everything about other faiths. Their practitioners can awaken Christians to aspects of their faith that get forgotten, especially the spiritual disciplines. In my essay on religions I explore how good people outside Christian faith qualify the unique revelation of God in Christ through evidence of holiness outside Christianity. To the cynical question 'Can religion lead you to God?' my elucidation is 'Yes, in the sense of religion expressing love in return for love'. In Christianity God leads us to God.

In understanding the Cross the idea of God willing his Son to suffer to make things right in the world raises so many questions for some people that they prefer living agnostic with the wrongs. My elucidation on God and the Cross works, mindful of absence of any official doctrine about how God and humanity are made one in Christ, to present a vision of God with loving sameness to us yet an inviting and awesome difference from us. It is allied to essays on sin and guilt. The essay on the empty tomb sheds light on how belief in the resurrection of Jesus stems from the faith of the church and an accumulation of evidence taken seriously by historians. There can be no knock down proof of a past event and that of the resurrection needs pondering alongside an openness to the wider metaphysical questions that spill out from it, especially Christ's divinity. Might not the most meaningful thing in life be what - or who - conquers death?

This essay notes how the Spirit-filled existence of Jesus after his resurrection went beyond resuscitation of his corpse to make him mandated source of eternal life for humankind. Such hope, looking beyond the physical order, fuels belief 'that all things work together for good for those who love God, who are called according to his purpose' (Romans 8:28).

'Elucidations: light on Christian controversies' addresses suffering and unanswered prayer in the context of the coronavirus pandemic which raises questions about the working for good of divine love and power mentioned by St. Paul. The pandemic has been a repressing force like a brake or imprisoning ball and chain. With an autobiographical slant my elucidations dwell on the paradox of praying to God to exercise his power to eradicate the virus whilst encouraging believers who suffer to trust God's working through it to a greater end. Frustration at unanswered prayer is presented at the highest level as disappointment that human beings are not yet aflame with love for God and one another evidenced in lack of justice and peace and disrespect for the environment. At the end of his book of this title Balthasar strikes a challenging note in addressing critics of institutional Christianity: 'Of course the Church 'should'… It 'should' do everything and much more than it ever can. I would simply like to know whether all those who leave the Church because it does not fulfil their expectations of it find satisfaction elsewhere. Whenever I hear, 'the Church should', then that simply seems to say to me, 'I should'. The more so because I receive so much more from the Church than I deserve. More than ever a man or a human society could give. It is up to me, up to us, to see that the Church comes closer to that which in reality it is'. Light on Christian controversy is most effective when it illuminates us so as to take this point and press on in 'the light of the knowledge of the glory of God in the face of Jesus Christ' (2 Corinthians 5:6b). (1)

John Twisleton

Feast of Pentecost 2021

1
Anti-Semitic?

We have close friends who are Orthodox Jews. They have been to Church with us and we have gone with them to Synagogue. In recent years our conversations have brought out ongoing sadness in the departure of several of their Jewish friends to Israel as a result of feeling at the sharp end of growing anti-Semitism in the UK. In one of his last 'Thoughts of the Day' on BBC in November 2019 the late Rabbi Jonathan Sacks said: 'A few days ago, two Jewish children were sitting with their parents in a train on the London Underground when a man came up to them and for almost twenty minutes harangued them with anti-Semitic abuse. Someone intervened but was threatened with violence. Then a young woman confronted the man, and calmly told him what he was doing was wrong. This distracted him and saved the day. It was a heroic act. The hero was a young Muslim woman wearing a hijab... That we in Britain should still be talking about anti-Semitism, Islamophobia, or racism at all, is deeply shocking. But it reminds us of the distance between public utterances of politicians and the reality, and it's been like that for a very long time... Racism has returned to Europe and to Britain - are we, and the politicians who represent us, doing enough to stop it? We still have to fight for the truth that every group should feel safe; and that our differences, not just our similarities, are what make us human. The Bible taught this in its opening chapter by saying that every human being is in the image and likeness of God. Meaning that one who is not in my image - whose colour, culture or creed is not mine - is nonetheless in God's image' (2).

Elucidating anti-Jewish sentiment risks being patronising as a non Jewish writer but I must proceed. Though I believe Christianity to be Pro-Jewish with a Jewish founder, I cannot deny the dark side of church history. Christian fuelling of anti-Semitism culminated in the murder of millions of Jews through the genocidal policies of Nazi Germany we call the

Holocaust. Christians down the ages preaching the love of neighbour whilst making an exception for Jews seems beyond our understanding but that contempt traces back to the start of the Christian Era. Rabbi Sacks quoted a text held sacred by both Jews and Christians, Genesis 1:27, as counter to anti-Semitism: 'God created humankind in his image, in the image of God he created them; male and female he created them'. Over the last half century the mainline churches have taken that text to heart rejecting the anti-Jewish contempt which had developed over centuries in Christian tradition. It is a volte face as welcome as it is extraordinary with a religion eating its words, even if such recent words are taking time to express themselves in more respectful action. Such action has now impacted the most sacred liturgy of Christians celebrated in Holy Week. In the past, there were near derogatory references to Jews as being instrumental in Christ's passion. Replacement prayers for Good Friday celebrate the Jews as God's ancient people, privileged to be first to hear his word, going on to ask for greater understanding between Christians and Jews.

The Founder of Christianity was a devout Jew, following Jewish Law whilst seeing himself as its fulfilment. Christ's death and resurrection revealed his divinity to initially Jewish followers making Christianity an innovation from monotheistic Judaism. In the early days Christians and Jews coexisted, sharing the Jewish scriptures, worshipping together with Christian input. The destruction of the Jewish Temple in 80 AD led to a re-invention of Judaism. The lost sacrificial culture was seen by Christians as fulfilled in the sacrifice of Christ. The same loss led to prioritising synagogue worship among Jews. As Christianity spread among non-Jews Christians and Jews separated into churches and synagogues and hostility grew between them. From a Christian angle, ritual laws such as circumcision came to be seen as unnecessary for salvation. From a Jewish angle, belief in Christ's divinity was blasphemous. In some accounts of Jesus' death the culpability of 'the Jews' was emphasised expressing contempt for blindness towards the coming of the Messiah and rejection of God's Son. The 2019 Church of England report on Christian-Jewish relations owns this sad legacy. 'Promotion of what has been called "the teaching of contempt" has fostered attitudes of distrust and hostility among Christians towards their Jewish neighbours, in some cases leading to violent attacks, murder and expulsion' (3). If we read through the New Testament as a whole it becomes clear Christ's sufferings and death were seen as willed by God on account of all humanity with the Jewish and Roman leaders who caused it his instruments. Though contempt for Jews as 'deicides' lamentably continued it was rivalled more profoundly by humble self-contempt among Christians as sinners 'for whom Christ died' (1 Corinthians 8:11). The same report quotes Archbishop Michael Ramsey: 'Those who crucified Christ are in the true mind of the Christian Church representatives of the whole human race, and it is for no one to point a finger of resentment at those who brought Jesus to his death, but rather to see the crucifixion as the divine judgement upon all humanity for choosing the way of sin rather than the Love of God. We must all see ourselves judged by the crucifixion of Christ'. (4)

Is it not anti-Jewish for Christians to evangelise Jews in the light of such history? UK Chief Rabbi Ephraim Mirvis believes so and his view is given prominence in an 'Afterword' published at the end of the recent C of E Report. Applauding the penitential tone, he criticises its affirming of evangelisation: 'even now, in the twenty-first Century, Jews are seen by some as quarry to be pursued and converted'. Mirvis makes a contrast with the 2015 Roman Catholic report which he says makes clear 'that the Catholic Church would 'neither conduct nor support any specific institutional mission work directed towards Jews"' (5). The quotation from that 2015 report is qualified however by the sentence which follows it: 'While there is a principled rejection of an institutional Jewish mission, Christians are nonetheless called to bear witness to their faith in Jesus Christ also to Jews, although they should do so in a humble and sensitive manner, acknowledging that Jews are bearers of God's Word, and particularly in view of the great tragedy of the Shoah' (6). The same report has a scripture text as heading from Romans 11:29 'The gifts and the calling of God are irrevocable'. The verse is part of St Paul's rich reflection on the ongoing existence of the Jewish community despite the coming of God in Christ. Though Paul acted forcefully against Christians before his conversion, and robustly towards Jews after encountering Christ, he came to reflect on the dignity of Judaism in these words. 'I have great sorrow and unceasing anguish in my heart. For I could wish that I myself were accursed and cut off from Christ for the sake of my own people, my kindred according to the flesh. They are Israelites, and to them belong the adoption, the glory, the covenants, the giving of the law, the worship, and the promises; to them belong the patriarchs, and from them, according to the flesh, comes the Messiah, who is over all, God blessed forever. Amen. (Romans 9:2-5)

In the face of the anti-Semitism of our age the Christian response is primarily one of penitence for any part in fuelling that base sentiment, expressed in both the Anglican and RC documents, allied to the resolve to act against it. At the same time evangelisation, key part of Christian identity, though not to be a matter of 'targeting' cannot exclude the Jewish community. It continues alongside the mutual presence and dialogue of communities increasingly at home with one another. Even the great evangelist St Paul accepted what he called the 'unsearchable... inscrutable ways' of God demonstrated in the two communities continuing alongside one another until Christ's return.

'For the gifts and the calling of God are irrevocable. Just as you were once disobedient to God but have now received mercy because of [Jewish] disobedience, so they have now been disobedient in order that, by the mercy shown to you, [the Jews] too may now receive mercy. For God has imprisoned all in disobedience so that he may be merciful to all. O the depth of the riches and wisdom and knowledge of God! How unsearchable are his judgments and how inscrutable his ways! "For who has known the mind of the Lord? Or who has been his counselor?" "Or who has given a gift to him, to receive a gift in return?" For from him and through him and to him are all things. To him be the glory forever. Amen' (Romans 11:29-36).

2
Being Pro-Life

'Does life begin at conception or birth? Neither - it begins when the children leave home!' It is good to hopefully get a laugh out of a serious matter that frequently sets Christians at loggerheads with their contemporaries. Thanks to medical science everyone is able to see what only God saw before, life in the womb, and that knowledge can be problematic. The use of ultrasound in obstetrics and gynaecology traces back to a paper in 1958 by Ian Donald, John McVicar, and Tom Brown "The investigation of abdominal masses by pulsed ultrasound" (7). This contained the first ultrasound images of an unborn child described there clinically as 'the foetus'. So many blessings have come to pregnant women from ultrasound scans and yet the information provided has led some parents into agonising decision making. Where handicap is evident, should the pregnancy proceed? Being 'pro-life' in a narrow definition is associated with accepting any unborn child as God's gift of a new life rejecting abortion. The label 'pro-choice' affirms a mother's right over her body including her right to destroy any foetus she is bearing if she judges their life prospects as weak or the birth as being against her own interests. Already the word 'life' is being used in two senses, one's existence and one's vitality. Being pro-life might be seen as about affirming the right to exist as well as the option to exist well or 'get a life'. In global politics the capital letter 'Pro-Life' lobby seem invariably linked to countering abortion and euthanasia rather than improving employment prospects and healthcare and their strong Christian backing can result in a misrepresentation of the witness of Christian Faith to God's special love for human beings in his image over the whole of their existence.

Mike and Sue were faced with a grievous decision after a scan showed their unborn child might be handicapped. They asked my advice and I encouraged them to accept what was in Sue as a precious gift from God who would give them help to continue as the good parents they already were. They agonised over the pregnancy, Sue especially, and decided for a termination. This involved Sue treating what was in her as an unwelcome growth for the short period before the abortion. Mike found this really difficult and their differences here contributed eventually to the failure of their marriage. I tell this story with names changed because I shared this couple's agony, besides being privileged at their request to clarify Christian teaching. I was upset about the decision but bent over backwards to be supportive to the family and still keep them all with the deceased child in my prayers. The experience made me more sympathetic to women faced with unwanted pregnancies or the prospect of caring for a disabled child. Through ultrasound scans we have an opportunity to protect and enhance life in the womb. We also gain information no past generation had which on occasion places parents on the horns of a grievous dilemma in which, like many choices in life, either outcome is unsatisfactory or tragic.

'For it was you who formed my inward parts; you knit me together in my mother's womb. I praise you, for I am fearfully and wonderfully made. Wonderful are your works; that I know very well. My frame was not hidden from you, when I was being made in secret' (Psalm 139:13-15a). Being pro-life captures the sense of that scripture and an advocacy for life wherever it is in jeopardy: in the womb, afflicted by injustice or vulnerable through old age. If life is God's gift its deliberate destruction is wrong in many situations even if that destruction is judged a 'lesser evil' as, classically, in warfare. The defence of life in the womb links to honouring what is seen as created in God's image, a human being with potential and not just a potential human being. There is deep irony though in how Christian involvement in politics sometimes majors on challenging abortion whilst shirking back from the need to address the poverty and social ills which impact the quality of life for many and contribute to forcing women to consider that option. Being pro-life in Christianity is inseparable from its Founder's stated aspirations which draw on the prophecy of justice in Isaiah and point to fullness of life as a gift of the indwelling Holy Spirit which is his gift to believers through baptism and faith: 'The Spirit of the Lord is upon me, because he has anointed me to bring good news to the poor. He has sent me to proclaim release to the captives and recovery of sight to the blind, to let the oppressed go free... I came that they may have life, and have it abundantly' (Luke 4:18 cf Isaiah 61:1, John 10:10b)

At the other end of pro-life advocacy is the countering of legislation allowing euthanasia which gives people the right to medical assistance in ending their lives when they see fit. In this countering Christians are in alliance with other groups and individuals who fear such legislation makes the elderly vulnerable to unscrupulous relatives and agencies. Why do people want to kill themselves? High profile cases relate unbearable physical, mental and emotional pain which make death preferable to life. In 2018 French Roman Catholic Bishops issued a declaration tellingly named, 'End of Life: Yes to the Urgency of Fraternity', in response to calls to allow euthanasia. The statement laments the scarcity of palliative care in France is inadequate but argued that euthanasia was no answer. Trust between doctors and patients would be undermined as professionals judged some lives as no longer worth living. 'Killing, even under the guise of compassion, can in no case be a cure'. People asking to die need supportive care 'attentive accompaniment, not a premature abandonment to the silence of death... It is a true fraternity that is urgently needed - it is the vital link of our society,' they said (8). Where people feel loved or 'in fraternity' they can come to value themselves all the more, agreeing with those who demonstrate to them how much they are loved. Love is the ultimate pro-life movement and assuager of pain but there is not enough love around and a great deal of loneliness in western society. These reflections should not subtract from our accepting the burden of pain many individuals feel which makes euthanasia seem to them a lesser evil.

'O God, from my youth you have taught me, and I still proclaim your wondrous deeds. So even to old age and gray hairs, O God, do not forsake me, until I proclaim your might to all the generations to come' (Psalm 71:17-18). Those words of the Psalmist capture the vitalising people gain from God across their years and beyond them in the resurrection. I recall visiting Peter in our local Hospice over the last year of his life and being impressed by his humour and joy in facing death. Before he died he made a recording for Premier Christian Radio series which included these words: 'I'm Peter Nicholson and I'm nearly 70. I'm in a Hospice and I have kidney failure but I'm not upset about it because I don't feel alone. Right from an early age I learned about Jesus and God and I was told then, and its remarkable how this has been with me all my life, that if I'm ever lonely or upset or in difficulties God said talk to him and in fact I did just that. I know I'm in a situation where I'm getting close to the end of my life and he's with me again and I feel relaxed and happy, and especially happy in the good company of friends who are extremely supportive and bring me joy. It seems funny to say you feel joyful when you're close to death but I do feel very joyful and almost excited at what I might be in for' (9). Being 'Pro-Life' with capital letters is perceived by some as countering what they see as more suitable to them as individuals. Where this Christian conviction is coupled to practical accompaniment of those at the sharp end of things it can be impressive. Adoption of the children of parents who go to full term with unwanted pregnancies, challenging unjust structures to improve the livelihoods of people and the hospice movement providing palliative care to the dying are examples of transformative pro-life action Christians are part of. As in Peter's testimony the experience of practical love like this love in family, friendship and the Church makes life convivial even in a Hospice and anticipates a quality of joyous living beyond this world.

3
Believing the Bible

When I read the Bible I see how hard belief is. Turning the other cheek and graciously going a second mile with people who compel you to do one mile are for scriptural literalists not for me, I think, as I have my cake and eat it. Whereas the credibility of the Bible seems damaged in my eyes by people defending its literal interpretation, my problems with believing the Bible are in reluctance to take literally what Jesus says when it challenges my self interest. Believing the Bible, though essential to my own life, has sadly been narrowed in the eyes of many to believing impossible things with the surrender of intellectual integrity. In America's culture war the term 'Bible-believing Christian' has been given pejorative association through falsehood, discrimination and inability to face the truth among Christian leaders. The association of biblical faith with narrow thinking is nothing new, but it contrasts with testimonies about the wide vista scripture opens as people see 'the light of the knowledge of the glory of God in the face of Jesus Christ' (2 Corinthians 4:6b). Through faith in Christ's death and resurrection the wide space of eternity comes into the present moment, the future into the present, which is the victory of faith (1 John 5:4).

Walter Nigg's biography of Francis of Assisi (1181/2-1226) captures how believing the Bible can bring vibrant light into the darkness of the world. 'A final experience brought St. Francis face to face with his ultimate goal. He attended Mass and heard Jesus' commission to his disciples: "Take no gold nor silver, nor copper in your belts, no bag for your journey, nor two tunics, nor sandals, nor a staff..." At the end of the service Francis went to see the priest, asked him to read again the passage from Scripture and then clapped his hands with unspeakable joy. "That is what I want, that is what I am looking for, that is what I will do with all my heart". In that moment all his perplexity vanished. He knew from now on what precisely he wanted to do, and for him there was to be no more vacillation. The words of the Gospel had clinched the matter. Filled with overwhelming happiness he longed with his whole heart for nothing other than to follow the word of the Lord and to embody and revivify it in his own life' (10). God has revealed himself in Jesus – this is the impact of Christianity – and Scripture holds before us both the record and ongoing impact of that revelation. The Bible points us to what Jesus has done for us by his death and resurrection and helps hold us to him. When we meet Jesus and put faith in him we begin to see our life as part of the Bible story. We find purpose and belonging in this world and hope for the world to come. In the Bible there is a promise from God that its text contains the truth necessary for salvation. When we read it or hear it read and explained we like Francis are reminded that truth is something shining into us from outside, challenging us, not just something we think out within ourselves. This is expressed in another way by Paul in 2 Corinthians when he says 'our sufficiency is of God...it is God who establishes us' (3:5, 1:21) and when he speaks of the church as 'the pillar and bulwark of truth' (1 Timothy 3:15). God's truth sets us free as it enfolds us through the Bible and the Church. 'Let the word of Christ dwell in you richly' Paul says, 'teach and admonish one another in all wisdom; and with gratitude in your hearts sing psalms, hymns and spiritual songs to God' (Colossians 3:16). It is in the infectious worship and fellowship of believers that the Bible opens itself up to people as the word of God.

Jesus is the definitive Word of God (John 1:1f) who opens us up to believing the Bible and trusting God's promises, provision and purpose in the orbit of his people. I can recall a time when scripture had little meaning for me. That changed when I came to experience the Holy Spirit after a time of crisis in my Christian life. Looking back I recognise how we can fail to see the relevance of Scripture until inner ears are opened by repentance, turning our attention away from the selfish things that drive us in life towards receiving the Holy Spirit afresh. 'All scripture is inspired by God and is useful for teaching, for reproof, for correction and for training in righteousness' (2 Timothy 3:16). People who take God at his word in scripture see Jesus changing their life by that same

Spirit. This may not turn them into Franciscan monks or nuns but receiving Scripture's great connector to human life, the Holy Spirit who gives life to the Church, demonstrates to recipients that there is no word of God without power. On 24 May 1738 Methodist pioneer John Wesley opened his Bible at 2 Peter 1:4 and read of God's 'precious and very great promises...through which we ...may become participants in the divine nature'. He trusted this promise. That evening he reluctantly attended a Christian meeting in Aldersgate, London. There he felt his heart 'strangely warmed' and received an assurance of salvation setting him off into an itinerant preaching ministry covering 20,000 miles a year. Almost everywhere he preached lives were changed, such was his trust in the promise that God would use him. Meeting Jesus is about hearing 'the truth that sets you free' (John 8:32). Whereas Plato taught a philosophy in which truth was to be sought Christianity presents truth as something we seek and something - someone - who also seeks us and speaks to us through the sacred writings assembled by the Church into what is called the 'Canon of Scripture'.

What about mistakes in the Bible? How is it that Christ's cleansing of the Temple is at the start of John's Gospel but at the end of the other three Gospels? All versions cannot be literally true. There is a mismatching, unless Jesus cleansed the Temple twice, which seems unlikely given its obvious consequence in his rejection by his people. The timing of that incident is part of its significance but Christians live with the ambiguity. It doesn't make the salvation Jesus came to bring false or wrong. Biblical truth is about coming one to one with God first and foremost. Many examinations of the Bible are fruitless because they are dealing with it shy of that engagement. Reading the sizeable library of books that is the Bible (from the Greek biblia, which means library) without a guide can be problematic. Like the Ethiopian eunuch helped to understand the Bible by Philip in Acts chapter 8 people very often need a guide to get into scripture. We discern a hierarchy in the truth as we live trusting the Bible. There is the unchangeable truth of Christ and then a whole series of teachings which have been interpreted differently in different ages. Take slavery or money lending or the leadership of women. In each case you need the Bible as a whole to interpret texts that seem at first reading to put a brake on developments that have seemed good to the Christian community like freeing slaves, allowing money lending or promoting leadership among women.

Over time some truths stated in the Bible have faded in significance and others have come alive. Think of the text in Matthew 27:25 where Saint Matthew records the Jewish crowd shouting 'His blood be on us and on our children'. In past ages this text was made the pretext for much cruelty towards Jews in Europe. Now it is Bible passages like the letter to the Romans Chapters 9 to 11 that guide a more constructive engagement of Christians with Jews in the wake of the holocaust. Another rather neglected text whose truth has become more and more important in recent years is Acts 1:8 'You will receive power when the Holy Spirit has come upon you; and you will be my witnesses'. People have been rediscovering the truth hidden in this verse and the associated passage about Pentecost over most of the last century, up to when the Holy Spirit was known in a much weaker sense as the Holy Ghost. Christians trust the Bible primarily for such encouragement to engage with the things that matter eternally – the saving relationship of human beings to God, Father, Son and Holy Spirit. We will always have questions about believing the Bible but the Bible will also always have its questions about us. So Mark Twain wrote with typical humour: 'Most people are bothered by those passages in Scripture which they cannot understand; but as for me, I always noticed that the passages in Scripture which trouble me most are those I do understand'.

4
Confession to a priest

Pascal said 'holiness is the church's most powerful influence'. People respond generously when they catch a vision of something like that worth going out of their way for. Kneeling before God and giving him your heart is going out of your way in the fullest sense. Many Christians are first brought to their knees by a personal encounter with Christ through holy people or by a direct experience of God. Others come more dutifully whilst being prepared for Confirmation and First Holy Communion. For myself it first came from someone asking me if I had ever thought about going to Confession and finding it hard to say no to the suggestion which seemed to have the force of the Holy Spirit behind it. It was the last thing I would have chosen to do in some ways but eventually I did it and have done it again and again ever since. Going to confession to a priest once made habitual is always a combination of duty and joy. Despite that joyous visionary start years back to the discipline I have nevertheless found myself going many a time out of dutiful trust in age old Christian wisdom. This invites us to give a regular account to God for our sins and receive the announcing of forgiveness over individuals who are sorry for their sins and grace serving a new start with God.

If there is a Christian distinctive, looking across the spectrum of religions and world views, is it not the forgiveness of sins? It links to belief in Jesus Christ as God's Son bringing by his death and resurrection what God alone can bring to sinful humanity. 'In Christ God was reconciling the world to himself, not counting their trespasses against them, and entrusting the message of reconciliation to us... we entreat you on behalf of Christ, be reconciled to God. For our sake he made him to be sin who knew no sin, so that in him we might become the righteousness of God' (2 Corinthians 5:19-21). Human beings who can achieve so much see those achievements continually undermined by their failings and many a time yearn for a new start. This reality is behind the loving action of our Creator coming among us as a human being, 'to be sin who knew no sin' so as to provide the forgiveness of sins, helping us turn the page, move forward and be made ourselves agents of reconciliation. Jesus died in our place to live in our place. The Son of God became Son of Man so children of men could be made children of God and live free. Not free from sin so much as free from sin's power, as well as the destructive powers of sickness, death and the devil. This freedom is a gift to be sought which the Apostles' Creed summarises as 'the forgiveness of sins, the resurrection of the body and the life everlasting' (11) Significantly, represented by the proximity of the forgiveness and resurrection clauses in that Creed, Jesus Christ gave authority for his disciples to pronounce the absolution of sins on Easter Day. 'If you forgive the sins of any, they are forgiven them' (John 20:23a).

Christians disagree about the ways you receive God's forgiveness. They all agree church members should make themselves accountable both to God and to their church. Some are happy to use the minister as an instrument of this. Others see this as introducing a go-between that could subtract from Christ. For twenty centuries the ministry of forgiveness, of freeing from sin has continued in his church. From Easter Day the risen Christ now invisible to us has made himself present through signs - water, bread and wine, oil, touch – we call sacraments. Whilst the sacraments of baptism and eucharist have Christ's clear authority the other sacraments are valued in the church, including the ministry of forgiveness. Many find in such signs the healing touch of Jesus. Jesus died and rose that we might be forgiven but to have significance to individuals that forgiveness has to be received and there is the divergence. The Christian view of the church has two main emphases that can be labelled catholic and reformed. Among the larger bodies, Roman Catholic and Orthodox, there is belief in the visible church as both part of the gospel and closely allied to the extension of God's kingdom. Among the more reformed bodies, Protestant and Pentecostal, there is belief in the church more as invisible and ideal. Here there is greater indifference about the visible order of the church and her sacramental continuity as, for example, through the apostolic succession of bishops. Whilst the catholic emphasis about receiving forgiveness does not deny God's availability at all times to forgive, the assurance of that forgiveness is seen as being primarily received through confession to someone ordained with authority to forgive individuals on God's behalf. The reformed emphasis is more on direct access to God in Christ with the assurance of forgiveness being based on the promises of scripture and experience of the Holy Spirit. 'If we confess our sins, he who is faithful and just will forgive us our sins and cleanse us from all unrighteousness' (1 John 1:9). Promises like these are claimed by individual believers after they have confessed their sins to God directly and privately. A link between catholic and reformed traditions is found in open confession in which individuals announce sorrow for specific sins at church gatherings as encouraged in the letter of James: 'Confess your sins to one another, and pray for one another, so that you may be healed' (James 5:16a). The practice of confession to the church leader developed in the early centuries of Christianity partly out of the practical difficulties, including scandal associated with open confession. It linked to a growing practice of spiritual accompaniment now found across both streams of Christian tradition with different names: spiritual direction, soul friendship etc

In my booklet 'Why go to Confession?' I give three reasons: 'to deal with my sins, to deal with my feelings of guilt and to renew my membership of God's family' (12). Confession to a priest is part of the continual stripping away and reclothing essential to the living out of our baptism. This is a stripping away of things like guilt, unbelief, indifference, selfishness and wastefulness unspectacular and taken for granted in the eyes of the world but bringing sorrow to God. Even if the devil - father of lies - is expert at making sin lurid and confession hypocritical those who draw close to God through this rite might know otherwise. 'Do you not know that all of us who have been baptised into Christ Jesus were baptised into his death? Therefore we have been buried with him into death, so that just as Christ was raised from the dead by the glory of the Father, so we too might walk in newness of life'

(Romans 6:3-4). When we confess our sins to God directly or in the presence of a priest we are doing to death our sinful nature and welcoming afresh the new nature given to us by the grace of the Holy Spirit. The emphasis in sacramental confession is on this welcoming, which is why talk of 'going to Confession' has recently given way to talk of 'welcoming the sacrament of reconciliation'. This makes the point that, as with all sacraments, the emphasis is upon what God gives in forgiveness more than on our own act of confession, costly and important as that is. The biblical image for the exchange is Christ's parable of 'The Prodigal Son' more properly called that of 'The Father's Love: 'I will get up and go to my father, and I will say to him, 'Father, I have sinned against heaven and before you...' 'Quickly, bring out a robe – the best one – and put it on him; put a ring on his finger and sandals on his feet. And get the fatted calf and kill it, and let us eat and celebrate; for this son of mine was dead and is alive again; he was lost and is found!' (Luke 15:18,22,23)

Why go to a minister and not directly to God? It is not either-or. When the lost son admitted sorrow for his sins he was embraced by his father. Imagine his coming home to a note on the table 'all is forgiven' rather than having that loving embrace? Sacramental confession helps many Christians to get that embrace and lose guilt through the assurance of forgiveness in a bible-based sign in which individuals are given a welcome home to God and his church through the minister. It complements the assurance of forgiveness given to all Christians through prayer and the promises of scripture.

5
Eco friendly?

'I prayed with my heart, everything around me seemed delightful and marvellous. The trees, the grass, the birds, the earth, the air, the light seemed to be telling me that they existed for man's sake, that they witnessed to the love of God for man, that everything proved the love of God for man, that all things prayed to God and sang his praise.' This description of prayer captures the sense of God in all things central to Christianity. It comes from the Russian classic 'Way of a Pilgrim' (13) which encourages repeating the Jesus Prayer 'Lord Jesus Christ, Son of God, have mercy on me a sinner' as aid to attaining the ability to 'pray without ceasing' (1 Thessalonians 5:17). As one who uses and has written about the Jesus Prayer I confirm its ability to make the one praying feel one with nature in their prayer (14). Given the enormity of the environmental crisis I find this sense of creation praising God in tension with its 'groaning in labour pains' awaiting 'be[ing] set free from its bondage to decay [to] obtain the freedom of the glory of the children of God' (Romans 8:21-22). Both passages, 'Way of a Pilgrim' and Romans, imply a link between the agony and ecstasy of nature and human beings in their origin and destiny as understood in Christianity. Thinking through the 'eco-friendliness' of Christian faith uncovers a number of weighty things to be balanced one with another: heaven with earth, dominion with stewardship, physical with spiritual, individual with collective, economic with political, strategy with serendipity and belief with practice.

Ecology is the science of our home (Greek: 'oikos') seen as our physical environment. Christianity, believing 'our homeland is in heaven' (Philippians 3:20), lives with a balancing act here which explains some historical short-falls in eco-friendliness. Though heavenly-minded gratitude for all that is, as in the 'Way of the Pilgrim' example, keeps people in the present moment more aware of others and of nature, living assured of heaven with contempt for earth has an opposite sense. It is telling that, despite generations of theological reflection, it took until 2015 for a Pope to give teaching on the environment as in 'Laudato Si'. In his encyclical Pope Francis is at pains to achieve the rebalancing of human dominion and stewardship of earth taught in Genesis: 'The harmony between the Creator, humanity and creation as a whole was disrupted by our presuming to take the place of God and refusing to acknowledge our creaturely limitations. This in turn distorted our mandate to "have dominion" over the earth (cf Gen 1:28), to "till it and keep it" (Gen 2:15). As a result, the originally harmonious relationship between human beings and nature became conflictual (cf Gen 3:17-19)' (15). The insight Christianity brings to human origins and shortfalls can help the educational task facing the international community faced with damage that affects every living organism through the global environmental crisis. Holding belief in the dignity of human beings as bearers of God's image goes hand in hand with belief in their falling well short of that dignity through sin. If dominion were not more comfortable to us than the selfless service of keeping the earth, that damage would have been lessened.

Is Christianity environment friendly? Inasmuch as it balances reverence for both physical and spiritual elements in life. Spillage of oil, leaking of chemicals into our rivers, acid rain, deforestation and burning off fossil fuels are an irreverent assault upon the physical environment. Catholic and Orthodox traditions have developed sacramental understanding of the physical world counter to this irreverence, seeing the spiritual conveyed through physical nature. Whilst not denying the immediacy of the Holy Spirit held in Evangelical and Pentecostal traditions they see the extending of the incarnation of God in Christ into the sacraments. Spiritual grace is given through the physical order as in the water of baptism, bread and wine at the eucharist, oil in anointing and through the action of laying on hands. As Pope Francis writes: 'It is in the Eucharist that all that has been created finds its greatest exaltation. Grace, which tends to manifest itself tangibly, found unsurpassable expression when God himself became man and gave himself as food for his creatures. The Lord, in the culmination of the mystery of the Incarnation, chose to reach our intimate depths through a fragment of matter. He comes not from above, but from within, he comes that we might find him in this world of ours... the Eucharist is also a source of light and motivation for our concerns for the environment, directing us to be stewards of all creation' (16)

In the understanding of the Eucharist across Christian traditions there is a potentially eco-friendly balancing of individual, collective and global. 'Though we are many, we are one body, because we all share in one bread' (1 Corinthians 10:17). 'The bread that I shall give for the life of the world is my flesh' (John 6:51b). With other religions and movements Christianity represents people in solidarity committed to the common good beyond the aspirations and actions of individual followers. The common good of the world is also served by farming, fishing, industry, technology, the means of communication, governments and all who contribute to the creation and distribution of wealth. Having an effective say about the means of wealth production, curbing damage to the environment in its process and just distribution of that wealth goes beyonds individuals. It is achieved by collective aspirations especially governments. The future of the environment depends on such balancing of economics and politics in service of the common good where Christian witness stands alongside others in championing those on the margins.

My own career has seen involvement with the indigenous people or Amerindians of Guyana, South America training priests for the vast interior of that beautiful land which has its heavily populated north coast on the Caribbean Sea. Over the years I have seen the indigenous people of Guyana's interior grow in confidence as a minority group through struggles with mining and logging companies hard to police in a vast forest land. The Church has helped and continues to help give voice to such minorities who, especially in the Amazon basin, stand on the front line of rainforest devastation with its human consequences. In solidarity with such groups and many others the Chair of the Anglican

Communion Environmental Network made the following statement on the environment: 'The Christian faith is certainly about personal salvation. But it is more than that: Christianity is first and foremost a concern for the whole of the created order - biodiversity and business; politics and pollution; rivers, religion and rainforests. The coming of Jesus brought everything of God into the sphere of time and space, and everything of time and space into the sphere of God. All things meet together in Him: Jesus is the point of reconciliation. Therefore, if Christians believe in Jesus they must recognise that concern for climate change is not an optional extra but a core matter of faith (17).

Christianity eco-friendly? In this question there is a weighing of a big cause alongside the world's biggest problem and how they connect. We have considered balancing heaven with earth, dominion with stewardship, physical with spiritual, individual with collective and economic with political. From our initial list of weighty things in need of balance we have left balancing strategy with serendipity and the obvious conclusion of tipping belief into practice in serving the environment. Serendipity, openness to all contained in the present moment, thrills from the opening quotation about an individual praying the Jesus prayer in solidarity with 'the trees, the grass, the birds, the earth, the air, the light'. Strategy has an eye to Christians planning corporately and with others to address the environmental crisis. This needs balancing by individuals laying hold of the world in serendipity, moment by moment, with humility and gratitude before God. Though church documents contribute to forming strategies for environmental renewal to be acted upon, the future shape of the world relies on individuals recovering humble living as addressed in Laudato Si':

"'The external deserts in the world are growing, because the internal deserts have become so vast'. For this reason, the ecological crisis is also a summons to profound interior conversion... whereby the effects of encounter with Jesus Christ become evident in [a Christian's] relationship with the world around... gratitude and graciousness, a recognition that the world is God's loving gift, and that we are called quietly to imitate his generosity in self-sacrifice and good works... the conviction that "less is more"... marked by moderation and the capacity to be happy with a little' (18)

JOHN TWISLETON

6
Elucidating God

Shortly after I was ordained priest I had a crisis of faith. I went back to where I had trained. It was a chance to work out what should happen next since I hardly believed in the reality of God anymore. While there I was taken under the wing of Fr. Daniel, one of the Mirfield monks. He gave me this advice: 'Maybe, John, it is not God who's gone but your vision of him. Why not pray an honest prayer, like, 'God, if you're there, show yourself. Give me a vision of yourself that's to your dimensions and not mine'. With nothing to lose I prayed Fr. Daniel's prayer over two cliff-hanging days. Then God answered. He chose a leaf on a tree in the monastery garden. I was walking along with no particular thought in my head when my eyes fell on the leaf and it was as if it spoke to me. 'He made you', the leaf seemed to say. I was bowled over. As I moved forward I saw the great Crucifix that stands in the garden. 'I made you. I love you', the figure of Jesus seemed to say. 'Father, Son...what about the Holy Spirit?', my mind was spinning. The Father was saying 'I made you', the Son 'I love you'. Could it be that the Spirit was saying 'I want to fill you'? A group of monks prayed for me to be filled afresh with the Holy Spirit and from that day forward God has seemed closer to me in people and nature as well as in church. Such an experience has helped me understand what it means to pray 'In the name of the Father, and of the Son and of the Holy Spirit. Amen'. It was as if my vision of God had grown too 'samey' and needed to get 'different' and only God could do that, the living God who speaks to anyone prepared to lend an ear to him. In reminding me 'I made you' God used a leaf to speak to me – a leaf out of his book of nature!

Elucidating God is the greatest of challenges but pushed for brevity we could choose two headings: 'God is different' and 'God is the same'. Before that two heading elucidation, to stop some turning the page, I need a paragraph on masculine imagery. God is bigger than gender but the images given to speak of God in the Bible like Father and Son are linked to the history of Jesus who taught us to pray to God as Father. That doesn't mean God is not our mother as well. Christianity is about what God reveals of himself, of Godself in one way of talking. The Church is authorised by scripture to speak of God as Father, Son and Spirit not Mother, Daughter and Spirit. Once you try to avoid such relational terms using for example Creator, Saviour, Sanctifier, you depersonalise God and miss his invitation to relate with him one to one with all the saints.

God is different from us and yet the same as us. We humans are individual persons but God is three persons in one God which goes beyond reason. That is the great thing about God - his frontiers are beyond ours so he can invite us into new territories by what he chooses to reveal to us. The supreme territory is the life of the resurrection. Because of its core historical events, in Christianity talk of God is inseparable from a vision of him beyond this world. Austin Farrer makes this plain in one of his sermons: 'You can equivocate for ever on God's very existence... but a God who reverses nature, a God who undoes death, that those in whom the likeness of his glory has faintly and fitfully shone may be drawn everlastingly into the heart of light, and know him as he is: this is a God indeed, a God almighty, a God to be trusted, loved and adored' (19). The Bible says 'God created humankind in his image, in the image of God he created them; male and female he created them' and the gift of reason is seen as the mark of that image within us. By reason we can evaluate the goodness, truth and beauty around us as pointing to God as being more of the same. Yet there are things our minds cannot grasp like suffering and death, people who forgive one another and the immensity of space. Such realities reveal themselves to us as being bigger than our minds or beyond reason.

God has sameness to us and difference from us. Since God is one in himself and one with us in Jesus Christ we can experience his sameness. He is our loving source and ending, our Father. We are the children he loves and wants to be with him for ever. God's sameness appeals to us as reasonable beings. Since God is revealed in history as Father, Son and Holy Spirit, three persons in one God, he is gloriously different from us, with space and power to bring all other persons into communion with himself. This space and power was revealed upon earth in a human life of 33 years. God's space, power and holiness is so different from ours it needed bringing to focus, so we could see it, through God becoming a human being in the person of Jesus. 'As a magnifying glass concentrates the rays of the sun into a little burning knot of heat that can set fire to a dry leaf or a piece of paper, so the mystery of Christ in the Gospel concentrates the rays of God's light and fire to a point that sets fire to the spirit of man'. So wrote the great Christian mystic and writer Thomas Merton (20).

I got into a conversation at a supermarket till. The young man at the till didn't go to Church but I'll not forget what he said: 'God's all powerful but they make him to be a wimping wimp!' This observation brought back to me a frequent complaint made by the great explorer Laurens Van der Post about the Church's domestication of God which might be behind non-attendance of folk like my friend at the till. The explorer wrote: 'One of the strangest ideas ever conceived is the idea that religion is the opium of the people, because religion is a call to battle.. human beings in their rational selves.. shy like frightened horses away from a God who is not the source of opium for people but a reawakening of creation and a transcending of the forces and nuclear energies in the human soul' (21).

Van der Post was imprisoned by the Japanese during World War Two and lived under the threat of execution. A date was set. The night before he records experiencing a tremendous thunderstorm outside his prison. He saw in this storm a strengthening as if from the awesome truth of a God so different he can raise the dead. The Japanese were not ultimately in control. The storm witnessed a greater than human power which in the end would decide all. He was spared execution. God's all powerful - may he forgive us for making him 'a wimping wimp'! May God also forgive those of us who put him into words and make him seem neat and tidy. Theology is putting together human words about a reality beyond words. It is necessary because God in Christ, so different from us, has made himself the same as us by taking flesh and bidding us write words about him. Scripture takes precedence over all such words, a library of inspired documents, presenting God as awesome yet accessible in Christ. All religions claim some sort of revelation of God. Hindus see many gods expressing affinity or sameness with ordinary life. Muslims see one God above and beyond us whose utter difference from us seems to exclude any sameness. Christians are in the middle with three persons in one God, a God who is personal like ourselves but also beyond us as the ground of our being. God for Christians is different from us not just because of what he says about himself through scripture - or to put it inclusively what God says about Godself - but on account of our experience of that difference as believers as I found in the monastery garden and the supermarket and Van der Post discovered in prison.

Elucidating God is a calling forth both of the light of reason and the light of faith which together lift us beyond ourselves into his praise. As the word of God written in the prophet Isaiah states: 'For my thoughts are not your thoughts, nor are your ways my ways, says the Lord. For as the heavens are higher than the earth, so are my ways higher than your ways and my thoughts than your thoughts (Isaiah 55:8-9).

7
Eucharistic controversy

'Twas God the word that spake it, He took the bread and brake it, And what the word did make it, That I believe and take it'. In twenty seven words Queen Elizabeth I devoutly summarises millions of words uttered and written about the presence of Christ in the bread and wine of the eucharist. Her words cleverly duck and dive around how the words of Christ are said over the bread and what actually happens to the bread. The beauty of the sentence is its stress on what the Bible says, capturing an emphasis of the English Reformation, whilst not attempting to reduce the categorical and presumed transformative words of Jesus, 'This is my body' (22). The Reformer Martin Luther held to the same biblical faith and fell out with the more radical views of Zwingli and Calvin which disowned any transformation of the eucharistic elements: 'Since we are confronted by God's words, "This is my body" – distinct, clear, common, definite words, which certainly are no trope, either in Scripture or in any language – we must embrace them with faith . . . not as hairsplitting sophistry dictates but as God says them for us, we must repeat these words after him and hold to them' (23).

The sixteenth century divisions over how we understand the eucharist are still with us. Roman Catholics, Anglicans and Lutherans are unable to receive Holy Communion together other than in exceptional circumstances laid down by RCs. Formal disagreement continues over how the presence and sacrifice of Christ are found at the eucharist although light has been shed on these issues by agreed statements in recent years. The physicality of the eucharist remains a stumbling block for Christians with some adoring the bread and wine as if God and others seeing them as bare symbols with their residue discarded after Communion. The relationship of the eucharist to the Cross is immediate for some and a visual aid to others. As in a court when a judge asks a witness to recall what happened, and the witness tells their memory, the Protestant eucharist is close to mental recalling of Calvary.

In the same court image, a judge can recall a witness, and it is that physical recalling of Christ which is closer to the Catholic view. This sees a special manifestation of Christ's presence in the elements at every mass and presentation of these elements to God in a renewed pleading of the body and blood of Christ offered sacrificially on Calvary.

'For I received from the Lord what I also handed on to you, that the Lord Jesus on the night when he was betrayed took a loaf of bread, and when he had given thanks, he broke it and said, "This is my body that is for you. Do this in remembrance of me." In the same way he took the cup also, after supper, saying, "This cup is the new covenant in my blood. Do this, as often as you drink it, in remembrance of me." For as often as you eat this bread and drink the cup, you proclaim the Lord's death until he comes' (1 Corinthians 1:23-26). In those words Paul recalls what he received from others to hand on to us, which we receive from him and the Gospel writers, in obediently celebrating the eucharist. Christianity's Founder ordained this sacrament so his followers might be able to engage with his sacrifice and presence. At the eucharist we join the showing forth of his eternal sacrifice before the face of God the Father, are fed with his sacred body and blood and made more into one body, the Church, the body of Christ. It is the recent recovery of this last aspect of the eucharist, building unity through Holy Communion, that highlights the visible disunity of Christians at this sacrament, whilst encouraging work and prayer towards full unity across denominations.

Disagreement about Christ's presence in the eucharist centres on how, if at all, the action makes him present in the bread and wine. Reformation differences here are being superseded by common recognition of Christ's being made present in the rite through the scripture and preaching as well as in his people since Jesus said 'where two or three are gathered in my name, I am there among them' (Matthew 18:20). Modern rites, Catholic, Anglican or Protestant, have recovered the importance of scripture, through an ecumenical lectionary, and the sign of peace which affirms Christ's presence within individual Christians assembled for worship. Catholic rites still centre on the elevation of the host (consecrated bread) and chalice but with a balancing veneration of the Gospel book as instrument of Christ's presence with his people. Differences over eucharistic sacrifice are now more hidden in the text of the eucharistic prayers used which now mention the self-offering of the people. The recovery of that emphasis, distinctive of Anglican tradition, helps build out from the relationship of the altar to Calvary into the lives of worshippers. An Anglican Bishop involved in a discussion about what if any was the key moment in the eucharist was very pragmatic. For him it was the moment worshippers pass out through the church door! The Anglican- RC statement on Eucharistic Doctrine section on 'The Eucharist and the Sacrifice of Christ' concludes with that emphasis on self-offering in worship:

'The eucharistic memorial is no mere calling to mind of a past event or of its significance, but the Church's effectual proclamation of God's mighty acts. Christ instituted the eucharist as a memorial (*anamnesis*) of the totality of God's reconciling action in him. In the eucharistic prayer the church continues to make the perpetual memorial of Christ's death and his members, united with God and one another, give thanks for all his mercies, entreat the benefits of his passion on behalf of the whole Church, participate in these benefits and enter into the movement of his self-offering' (24).

Though Anglican eucharistic liturgy bears the scars of the Reformation with the studied ambiguity of some prayers, unlike RC prayers, it keeps an important emphasis on both Christ's sacrifice and Paul's call for believers 'by the mercies of God, to present your bodies as a living sacrifice, holy and acceptable to God, which is your spiritual worship' (Romans 12:1) . Eric Mascall makes this constructive summary: 'To the question which has caused so much dispute among Christians: 'Is anything offered in the Eucharist, and if so who offers what?' the all-inclusive answer is not just 'Jesus offers himself' or 'Jesus offers us' or 'We offer Jesus' or 'We offer ourselves' or 'We offer bread and wine', but 'The Whole

Christ offers the Whole Christ', an answer which can be seen to include, in their right places and proportions, all the others' (25). Mascall's synthesis echoes the age old Orthodox liturgy which pleads at the consecration: 'We offer you your own from your own in all things and for all things'. A similar understanding is stated in that last sentence of the Anglican-RC statement quotation on the nature of the eucharistic sacrifice, that we 'enter into the movement of Christ's self-offering'.

If any synthesis is possible from the five century eucharistic controversy it might be in this missionary aspect. Jesus uses our participation in the eucharist as a means of bringing us and the world into what he wants them to be. As the Orthodox priest and author Alexander Schmemann expresses it: 'When man stands before the throne of God, when he has fulfilled all that God has given him to fulfil, when all sins are forgiven, all joy restored, then there is nothing else for him to do but give thanks. Eucharist (thanksgiving) is the state of perfect man. Eucharist is the life of paradise. Eucharist is the only full and real response of man to God's creation, redemption and gift of heaven. But this perfect man who stands before God is Christ. In him alone all that God has given man was fulfilled and brought back to heaven. He alone is the perfect eucharistic being. He is the eucharist of the world. In and through this eucharist the whole creation becomes what it always was to be and yet failed to be' (26). Day by day Christians have an invitation to participate in a blessing and distribution of bread and wine that impacts the cosmos through the eucharistic sacrifice of Jesus who died in our place and comes here and now, there and then, to be in our place and that of the whole world before our Father. His institution of the eucharist calls forth obedience - 'do this in remembrance of me' - but more profoundly obedient self-offering in his own for our salvation and that of the whole world. 'See, God, I have come to do your will, O God' (Hebrews 10:7).

8
Evolution and the Bible

'I once had a go at the Bible but it's fiction from page one' they say. More than once I've wished the poetic account of creation came later so as not to be the hurdle it is to the literal minded. Ironically Genesis 1-2 both closes and opens to the literal minded, leading some to see its six day account of creation as literally mistaken and others to see every God-breathed letter as true. In an age of fake news, reported events are suspect and scripture's authoritative creation narrative is seen by literal minded cynics as clashing head on with scientific knowledge. By contrast literal minded faith resounds with reverence of Christians down the ages for the very words of the Bible but is unsupported by the mainstream of 21st century Christianity who honour scripture in a wider context. It is difficult for such Christians to see their fellows idolising the Bible, taking issue with evolution, in defence of what humans should never have to defend, the word of God no less, whilst reducing it to the literal text of scripture. 'In the beginning when God created the heavens and the earth, the earth was a formless void and darkness covered the face of the deep, while a wind from God swept over the face of the waters. Then God said, "Let there be light"; and there was light' (Genesis 1:1-3). Whilst people criticise this text, questioning who could be the reporter, others see its poetic form as first of seven stanzas putting the indescribable into words that tally with the scientifically accepted 'Big Bang' and a sequence of historically proven events. The explosion of light starts a sequel with water, land, plants, living and then thinking creatures. 'So God created humankind in his image, in the image of God he created them; male and female he created them' (Genesis 1:27). To hold Christian faith requires no surrender of intellectual integrity, or impossible defences, on account of this idea of being in God's image, with God-given minds, able to contain somewhat the question of our origins illuminated for 150 years by evolution theory. The truth of Christ, living word of God, the anchor that holds us is also the greatest clue to the forward movement and fulfilment of the universe.

How do Christians square the theory of evolution with scripture? We square the two by getting to grips with the heart of what both scripture and evolution theory really say. I say 'the heart' because if the biblical accounts of creation in Genesis need interpretation so does evolution theory. We don't have to choose between God bringing everything we know into being in days or billions of years of natural selection. Most churches accept we need care in interpreting the Bible lest we end up doing the impossible – defending God! Many scientists are unhappy with the idea of evolution disproving God because they see this theory homaging his purpose in creation reflected in the Genesis poem. The term evolution used in biology refers to the process by which new species of living things develop from pre-existing forms generation by generation. This process means organisms inherit features from their parents through genes. Changes or mutations in these genes can produce a new trait in the offspring of an organism. If a new trait makes offspring better suited to their environment, they will be more successful at surviving and reproducing. This process is called natural selection, and it causes useful traits to be made more common. Over many generations, a population can acquire so many new traits that it becomes a new species. This understanding of evolutionary biology grew from the 1859 publication of Charles Darwin's 'On the Origin of Species'. In addition, Gregor Mendel's work with plants helped to explain the hereditary patterns of genetics leading to an understanding of the mechanisms of inheritance. At first sight the opening pages of scripture contradict this description speaking of six days of creation against the evolution of life over four billion years. There is a plain challenge here about how Christians believe the Bible is true. How do Christians answer? By saying it depends what sort of truth you are talking about. Truth that's scientifically accurate? Historically precise? Or truth to get your life into gear! Christians believe in Jesus more than they believe in the Bible. It is the scriptural witness to Jesus and all he offers the human race that matters most. Saving truth matters more urgently than scientific or historical truth, though all truth matters in the end. Christians believe scripture cannot be mistaken as it presents the good news of Jesus to honest seekers of the truth as which is what the Bible says of itself in 2 Timothy 3:15 'the sacred writings are able to instruct (us) for salvation through Jesus Christ''. 'Can you trust the Bible?' The answer is 'Yes, you can'. Its truth is demonstrated in trustworthiness found by millions through the ages.

In Genesis, as in many other places, scripture talks in poetry whilst science is generally bound to accounting in prose. The Bible talks not of the mechanical laws of the universe but of who is behind the universe and what God's plan is for us all. By contrast evolution theory shows a purpose and direction to human history that should puzzle any atheist. So much so people now talk about 'atheism in the gaps', or the need for atheists to tackle the consensus of today's science that there is an order and direction and by implication a purpose to life on earth. How do Christians square evolution theory with what the Bible says? There are the two approaches. One that effectively denies evolution and one that accepts it with qualifications. Some Christians go as far as to suggest God has allowed fossils to test our faith rather than to point us to his genius in making an evolving world. They cannot accept any challenge to the literal interpretation of scripture perhaps because any other interpretation would give Christian tradition more authority than scripture. The other approach more widely accepted is to see scriptural truth as part of the Christian consensus of faith and as being of a different kind to scientific truth. Science deals with how things are made whilst the Bible deals with why things were made. Scripture and its God given supplement, nature, are to be taken together and not allowed to be rival interpreters of reality. On this view creation is presented as something ongoing rather than as simply an event in the past.

The French priest scientist and mystic Teilhard de Chardin taught from the first chapters of John's Gospel, Colossians and Hebrews how Christ holds all things in being and is bringing all things together in himself. Thinking from these scriptures he came to see the cosmos as like a cone with movements within it converging upon Jesus as the apex or omega point. Our individual futures, the future development of the church and the whole creation rests in Jesus and is to end in Jesus. Meditating on scripture Teilhard prophesied the connecting up of human consciousness we now experience in the global internet. Building as the scientist he was from the theory of evolution his work was initially controversial in church circles. His logical examination of the trajectory of evolution from inanimate matter to animation then human self-consciousness extrapolated to the cosmos being made incandescent with the glow of a single thinking envelope. This trajectory goes with Darwinian theory up to a point then radically diverges towards the Christian vision, where the God-given human capacity to converge and unify leaps beyond the materialist vision of 'survival of the fittest'. In Teilhard's thinking the global meeting of minds, as we now experience in the internet, would be the last stage before the uniting of holy hearts and souls in the communion of saints at Christ's return. In this process the exercise of human freedom, as in repentance and faith, is essential since the spiritual momentum of Christianity, carrying beyond the physical and psychological to God in his holiness, respects the human option to choose God or not (27). Christian faith which honours the Bible requires no surrender of intellectual integrity faced with scientific discoveries on the question of our origins based on evolution theory. As Teilhard demonstrates, the truth of Christ is in itself evolutionary, the greatest clue to the forward development of the universe. There remains an ongoing challenge from the dialogue of communities of faith with the scientific community to re-imagine the authority of the Bible across denominations. That authority rests over the whole body of Christians inviting their agreement in faith assisted by 'the Spirit of truth...who leads into all truth' (John 16v13). As surely as truth is one, the biblical witness to the divine plan to bring all things in the universe together in Christ is inseparable from the scientific uncovering of truth which, when guided by moral principle, serves the best development of humanity, the world and the cosmos.

9
Experience of the Holy Spirit

Years back I experienced the Holy Spirit in a Leeds Church. I came late to the service and as I came through the door heard loud harmonious singing without intelligible words. I fell to my knees awed by something so out of this world with hundreds of worshippers going with the flow of a holy humming successively rising and falling then dying down to silence. After that silence I heard one or two voices speaking words of consolation as if from God to the gathered worshippers along the lines 'I love you… I have a way forward for you… trust in Me'. It left an impression deep in my soul sowing the seed of being open to the Holy Spirit's gifts of tongues and prophecy mentioned in scripture.

A young couple came to see me who had fallen in love at their workplace. Both were already married and one of their existing partners was awaiting the birth of their first child. As Christians they insisted their relationship was from the Holy Spirit who had led them together. Discouraged by their respective Christian networks they hoped that, as a priest who visited their workplace, I might help them. It was an awkward inconclusive hour in which I had to point out how guidance for Christians involves both the Holy Spirit and scripture. Adultery I suggested was unlikely to be inspired by the Holy Spirit since God's Spirit and God's word are one. We parted sadly.

Both stories speak of subjective experience of the Holy Spirit, one encouraging and the other challenging. My experience in the Leeds Church showed me a wider sense of the Spirit's working in worship beyond opening up the meaning and power of scripture and sacrament which normally take centre stage focussed upon lectern and altar. Being among worshippers singing in tongues reminded me Christian worship is not just something we see before us but something that wells up from participants as we 'present our bodies as a living sacrifice, holy and acceptable to God, which is our spiritual worship' (Romans 12:1). The pastoral encounter with the couple by contrast found me introducing objectivity into a situation in which experience of the Holy Spirit seemed close to delusion. It took courage from them to approach me. I prayed a lot for them afterwards and do not know what outcome they found. They made me wiser about the difficulties people can face when experience of the Holy Spirit is familiar.

Throughout church history people have been inspired and confounded by the experience of the Holy Spirit. The Acts of the Apostles is a whole book about such inspiration given to disciples and how it confounds particularly those opposed to Christianity. Sometimes it is believers who get confounded there as with the leading given by the Spirit to include Gentiles (non-Jews) in the Church on the same terms as Jewish believers. The first Church Council prefaces guidance on this inclusion by saying authoritatively 'it has seemed good to the Holy Spirit and to us' (Acts 15:28). The consensus of believers about doctrine is seen as an objective work of the Spirit Christ promised would guide disciples 'into all the truth' (John 16:13). In his teaching on the use of the Holy Spirit's gifts of tongues and prophecy in Christian worship Paul is at pains both to encourage use of these gifts and to ask for them to be exercised with an eye to the consensus of believers under the authority of church leaders. 'God is a God not of disorder but of peace... [in worship] all things should be done decently and in order' (1 Corinthians 14:33,40). Earlier in that letter Paul presents the building up of love in the Christian community as the purpose behind experiencing the gifts of the Spirit which are to be used with an eye to enriching rather than disordering worship.

Through the Christian centuries prophets have been raised up to challenge hypocritical 'holding to the outward form of godliness but denying its power [the Holy Spirit]' (2 Timothy 3:5). They have done so by virtue of their direct experience of God. Such experiences have been vitalising yet controversial. Catherine of Siena lived in the 14th century when the church was much in need of reform. Her experience of the Spirit led to fearless countering of hypocrisy despite opposition. 'We've had enough exhortations to be silent' she said. 'Cry out with a thousand tongues - I see the world is rotten because of silence'. Anglican priest John Wesley similarly experienced the Spirit in 1738 when his heart was 'strangely warmed'. Though the eucharist was central to his life he held services with testimonies to personal experience of the Spirit. Bishop Joseph Butler asked him to leave his diocese questioning the authenticity of such experience saying famously: 'the pretending to extraordinary revelations and gifts of the Holy Spirit is a horrid thing - a very horrid thing!' Despite being a defender of divine intervention, stoutly opposing the 'deism' of his day that saw God remote from humanity, Butler opposed the Methodist movement with its stress on the experience of God as heretical contributing to the separation of the movement from the Church of England by Wesley's followers.

The way people talk about their experience of the Holy Spirit can indeed offend even if church life without experience of God can be deadening in its unspiritual formality. Theologians have struggled to find language to help people with experience of the Spirit to talk about it without seeming arrogant in having a direct-line to the Lord. 14th century Gregory of Palamas introduced a helpful distinction between God's energies, which we experience by his Spirit, and his essence which lies beyond human knowledge. It rings true to contemporary psychology in that though we know and experience people closely, especially our spouses, there always remains about them what is unknowable or known to them alone. My own readiness to experience the Holy Spirit, deterred historically by a perception of the emotional excesses of Pentecostalism, was helped by this insight dear to Eastern Orthodoxy which came into its own following a faith crisis. I had gone on retreat with the advice to ask God to give me a vision of himself more to his dimensions and less to the narrow, dull image I then possessed. There was an answer to this prayer which involved a sense of in-filling by the Holy Spirit which within weeks involved the experience of praying in tongues. A friend who had this experience reassured me the experience was true to the faith and prayer of the church through the ages. He pointed me to an insistence in the Orthodox Philokalia on inviting the prayer of the mind to become the prayer of the heart (28). I read this book, which later became a resource for discovering the Jesus Prayer. At the same time I read a book by Roman Catholic priest Simon Tugwell, 'Did you receive the Spirit?' which provided similar assurance that St Francis and the Cure d'Ars, two of my saint heroes, let alone Pope John XXIII evidently spoke in tongues (29). Through such study I came to see tongues as a love language granted the soul in answer to prayer, a gift that is subject to the will and, in Christianity at least, no evidence of derangement or hysteria. Further study using Kilian McDonnell & George Montague 'Christian Initiation and Baptism in the Holy Spirit' helped me see my experience of filling as completing my infant baptism (30). A helpful analogy is that of the relationship of its pilot light to a gas fire. Infant baptism lights the Spirit within whilst awaiting faith to grow so as to bring a Christian fully aflame with the Spirit. This insight has helped me invite others to seek the experience of baptism or filling in the Spirit as something optional yet vital linked to the faith and life of the church through the ages east and west.

Controversy about the experience of the Holy Spirit has not deterred the growth of both Pentecostalism and the Charismatic Movement in mainline churches such that a good section of the 21st century church owns this experience. 'Charismatics' in major denominations submit to a church authority which oversees a broader spectrum of spirituality than their own and through that submission many have risen to be inspirational pastors. Just as the Acts of the Apostles chronicles the spreading of the Gospel through such experience, recognition of God's transforming presence in our lives and wanting to engage more fully with that and share with others about it is a key to Christian mission. Opening up to the transforming power of the Spirit is nothing anti-intellectual or anti-institutional as many see it but rather a servant of the truth that is in Jesus and of bringing Christian communities more fully alive. 'You will receive power when the Holy Spirit has come upon you; and you will be my witnesses' (Acts 1:8)

10
Gay Christians

'Homosexual people have a right to be in the family. They are children of God. They have a right to a family. Nobody should be thrown out of the family or made miserable over this. What we have to make is a law of civil coexistence, for they have the right to be legally covered. I stood up for that' Pope Francis said recently (31). The discrimination against homosexual persons over the Christian centuries is being happily reversed so that in our society persons holding to the historic Christian prohibition of same sex physical relations are feeling the pinch. Until 1967 the Christian ethic was upheld in legislation but now it is those who teach it that must watch their step. In elucidating this controversial area the main thing to point out is how wrong it is to discriminate against persons be they gay or Christian or whatever. This is for Christians a matter of justice flowing from the day to day praying of 'Our Father' which affirms God's indiscriminate love for all. Discrimination against wrong behaviour is another matter and on that there are inevitable disagreements in a multicultural society which are settled by legislation. Not all Christians see this distinction within the makeup of discrimination and some fall well short of their Lord's call to love their neighbour whatever their belief or behaviour. On stated belief at least many Christians nowadays go with the saying 'I disapprove of what you say, but I will defend to the death your right to say it'.

Working as a cover priest, particularly in Brighton, I am aware from parishioners how gay Christians can feel caught in a cross fire, suffering alienation from both fellow gays and fellow Christians. Both networks take pride in inclusivity but through the ignorance of one group about the other people get caught on the sharp edges of both. Brighton & Hove Pride Festival promotes itself as 'a dazzling display of inclusivity' in which the Lesbian Gay Bisexual Transgender Queer (LGBTQ) community campaigns for increased freedom from discrimination allowing them to live life on an equal footing with non LGBTQ folk. Many Churches also exhibit a 'dazzling display of inclusivity' making space for friendships to grow between heterosexual and homosexual, married and celibate, young and old, rich and poor, employed, retired, unemployed and so on. On occasions like Pride Sunday some Churches especially rejoice with their gay members as they seek to become more fully what God has made us to be, coming 'to the measure of the full stature of Christ... speaking the truth in love we must grow up in every way into him' (Ephesians 4:13,15). That sort of growth - towards citizenship of heaven - comes as we grow more rooted in apostolic faith, in the soil of holy church, so we blossom not just in our humanity but in divinity, in holiness. Our sexual orientation in the Christian view is second to living lives oriented to Jesus Christ, loving him and aspiring to make him loved. The friendship and understanding described is in many a Christian congregation and vitalises mission as it builds up through 'speaking the truth in love'.

Here are six truths of Christian faith to ponder in the controversial and sensitive realm opened up to us by gay church members distilled from my own pastoral encounters over the years.

First all love is of God, love between friends, husbands and wives, parents and children and we all need more love in our lives so we can grow into 'the full stature of Christ'.

Second Scripture applauds same-sex friendship as for David and Jonathan in the Old Testament and those between Our Lord and his apostles, especially Saint John.

Third the Christian tradition is historically opposed to the sexualising of friendship, in particular physical sexual activity outside of marriage.

Fourth the Sacrament of Marriage is recognised as a divine ordinance in which the 'delight and tenderness of sexual union' (Common Worship) between husband and wife mirrors Christ's love for the Church and the love of the Father for the Son in the Holy Spirit.

Fifth same-sex marriage has no basis in scripture or Christian tradition which affirms heterosexual marriage as 'the foundation of family life in which children are born and nurtured' (Common Worship). Sexual intercourse effects life-giving love with inseparable unitive and procreative aspects.

Sixth Jesus starts his Sermon on the Mount by warning against lust. 'I say to you that everyone who looks at someone with lust has already committed adultery with them in their heart' (Matthew 5:28). Our sexual preferences are incidental to the great failing of treating anyone as an object even in our hearts.

Such principles of the faith of the church through the ages inform the church's pastoral ministry, a ministry of care shared by all Christians and not just the clergy (32). To earth these truths here are some pastoral examples with names changed.

I think of Steve, a young man who holds to these principles who has been an active member of a political party. He told me he was thinking of a career change because his Christian views were increasingly alien to his Party making him unselectable. He needed my care and encouragement in holding to his faith.

Then Miriam in a same sex relation with twins who in talking to me informally about their baptisms asked me whether the church could approve their parents' union. In that conversation I left the door open for the delightful infants, affirmed marriage by nature as a physical union of man and woman and offered an informal prayer for the couple with new responsibilities.

Joe who is gay talked to me about his possible call to the priesthood. I advised him to be honest about his state of life in the discernment process and courageously face up to the Church of England House of Bishops guidance that, I quote, on account of 'the distinctive nature of their calling, status and consecration' the clergy 'cannot claim the liberty to enter into sexually active homophile relationships'.

Sally is a Lesbian active in her Church who has to deal with a lot of hassle from friends in the LGBTQ community because of her faith. A report by gay rights charity Stonewall has underlined the bullying LGBTQ people face from those within and outside of their community. It is estimated one in ten gay Christians face Sally's trauma.

Whether we find ourselves attracted to the opposite sex or our own sex most of us did not choose one or the other but just discovered it as the way we are. There is now strong evidence that homosexual orientation is fixed early in life, maybe before birth, out of our control and no counselling or therapy can change it. Nevertheless many gay people encounter prejudice so that legislation against such discrimination has rightly come about. The Gay Pride movement has much Christian support but it is paradoxical. Pride is the sin that cuts you off from God on account of determined and aloof self sufficiency. For LGBTQ people pride's opposite is not humility though but *shame*. A movement of inclusion to counter such shame about the way you are is wholly laudable. At the same time losing shame about how you are does not absolve gay people from accountability for the way you live your life, especially if they are Christians, as the teaching and examples above attempted to elucidate.

Many Christians worked in the 1960s to decriminalise homosexual behaviour in the UK whilst retaining belief in its sinfulness. To shape law to give a right for some to behave in what others see as being wrong is the consequence of Christian teaching on justice. The law can give a right to something without actually making it right. If the legal establishment of Christian teaching has oppressed gay people in the past the shoe is now very much on the other foot in Britain. A teacher who commends marriage or celibacy in accordance with Christian teaching but refuses to commend a physical same-sex relationship is now vulnerable to anti-discrimination laws. If Christians have arguments with homosexuals about sexual activity, they have the same arguments with heterosexual people who choose cohabitation rather than marriage. The recently published Church of England resource on sexuality expands on this and many perceived inconsistencies in pastoral care (33).

Christianity is for those oriented towards both the same or opposite sexes but the 'orientation' that matters most in sexual morality is for Christians that towards God. Only by God's grace can any of us harness our sexual powers and see them transformed by God towards self-giving love. We all live in need of mercy. Our sense of our need of mercy is our strongest witness to those in our circle living without the belonging, purpose, empowerment, and forgiveness Jesus Christ brings to people irrespective of their sexual orientation. It is orientation through him to the all embracing, indiscriminate love of God that puts all on common, level ground at the foot of the Cross.

JOHN TWISLETON

11
God and the Cross

'If it were true it would be cosmic child abuse' I've heard in and outside Christian circles in response to the understanding of God's love shown in the Cross. The idea of God willing his Son to suffer and die to make things right in the world raises so many questions for some people that they prefer living agnostic with the wrongs. That there is no official doctrine of atonement - how God and humanity are made one in Christ - makes for another complication. So does the simplification of thinking on the Cross to throw a line to Christian seekers not to mention poetic licence employed in hymns about the passion of Christ. Evangelical songwriter Stuart Townend weathered criticism for these lines in his hymn In Christ Alone: 'on that cross, as Jesus died, the wrath of God was satisfied' (34). At the other side of the Christian spectrum this phrase in a Roman Catholic prayer has detractors: 'Look, we pray, upon the oblation of your Church and... the sacrificial Victim by whose death you willed to reconcile us to yourself' (35). The same talk of God satisfying justice through sacrificing his Son is found in the middle of the Christian spectrum in an Anglican text, the Book of Common Prayer, which speaks of Christ's 'full, perfect, and sufficient sacrifice, oblation, and satisfaction, for the sins of the whole world'. Where is God's love in the suffering of Jesus? Jesus died in our place to live in our place. Such a sentence is daring, as a throw away line to seekers, linking the death of Christ to his resurrection and the gift of the Holy Spirit received by repentance, faith and baptism. So much is at stake here there needs to be daring, daring that reflects the divine mind 'for God so loved the world that he gave his only Son, so that everyone who believes in him may not perish but may have eternal life' (John 3:16). Though words crack speaking of God, the good news of Christianity comes in words unpacking two events and one to come - God's making, redeeming and completing the cosmos - which all creatures are caught up with willingly or unwillingly. Of the three events only one, the life, death and resurrection of Jesus, is fully graspable. The 'Big Bang' of creation is less so let alone the promised return of Christ and God's being made 'all in all... bringing many children to glory' (1 Corinthians 15:28, Hebrews 2:10). Because we are actually part of this divinely willed process we have no clear insight on what we or the cosmos are about, save what has been revealed to us by God which is, precisely, the good news of Jesus Christ as Saviour and Lord. The daring action of God is in making all things knowing they would not work out well once humans came upon the scene, and providing the remedy in Jesus, God and man, to lead the partnership which is his Church, the human and divine agency set to effect his overall purpose to bring all things to completion in Christ (Ephesians 1:3-14).

Seeing God's love in the suffering of Jesus is inseparable from seeing that action plan in which it is central, providing in the Cross the symbol loved and derided in the world up to today. The derision that such suffering would make God abuser of his Son links to widespread acknowledgement in our society of the evil of child abuse through the ages. Ironically this recognition is not unrelated to Christian insight into human dignity, the valuing of 'weak brothers and sisters for whom Christ died' (1 Corinthians 8:11). The loving action of God sending his Son to suffer goes back to the design of creation and its intended redesign in Christ to make eternal friendship with God possible by dealing with what breaks that friendship. 'Christ himself bore our sins in his body on the cross, so that, free from sins, we might live for righteousness; by his wounds you have been healed' (1 Peter 2:24).Jesus died in our place to live in our place so when we come repeatedly to the Cross our sinful nature is repeatedly put to death and the life of his Holy Spirit repeatedly gains power within us. The conflict of such powers is evident to people who put faith in Jesus and it traces back to the impact of the crucifixion when 'the earth shook and the rocks were split' (Matthew 27:51). Priest poet Raneiro Cantalamessa writes: 'In the Alps in summer, when a mass of cold air from the north clashes with hot air from the south, frightful storms break out disturbing the atmosphere; dark clouds move around, the wind whistles, lightning rends the sky from one end to the other and the thunder makes the mountains tremble. Something similar took place in the Redeemer's soul where the extreme evil of sin clashed with the supreme holiness of God disturbing it to the point that it caused him to sweat blood and forced the cry from him, "My soul is sorrowful to the point of death... nevertheless Father, not my will but yours be done."'

God's willing the suffering of his Son is unintelligible to any human parent unless linked to God's wishing the best for us as the holy ground of our being. God, who is different to us in holiness, made us, with a sameness to God in love, for eternal friendship. Hence decisive action, at one point in time, to reveal the victory of holiness over sin, opening access to Christ's victory for us here and now. Through prayer and sacrament that victory brings cleansing and renewal into lives and communities. Jesus is seen again and again acting against evil, rescuing people from its destructive power when they seek him at the Cross. The spread of evils such as social inequality, unjust trade, wars and so on are linked to the misuse of free will. A loving God, despite his holiness, is bound to allow evil so as to respect this freedom. Christians misuse free will just like non-Christians. They get sick and die like anyone else. They also experience a countering of destructive powers such as sin, sickness and death when they seek their Lord. The death and resurrection of Christ are found to counter the powers of evil when the risen Lord is given freedom to do so in lives opened up to him.

Where is God's love in the suffering of Jesus? When the hymn speaks of 'the wrath of God being satisfied' by Christ's suffering on our behalf it is a wrath against sin not against his Son. It is hate, not wrath, which is the opposite to love, something taught us in family life. A mother had a son she loved very deeply. He was a tearaway and always let her down. One day he commits a shameful act and is filled with guilt at his sin. How does that mother feel at the evil which has gripped her dearest one? What agonies that mother bears at the shame her son has brought upon himself holding wrath against the wrongdoing. The mother suffers far more than her son who is not holy or loving enough to register the evil. In the suffering and death of Christ God's heart breaks for us. Can we imagine what our sins, which we barely repent of, are doing, have done to Almighty God in his great love for us? God is our holy parent who made us so how unacceptable to him must be the sin that clings to us and how great must be his wrath against it? 'Holy, holy holy is the Lord, God of power and might' (Isaiah 6:3). Pride, anger, envy, prayerlessness, bitterness, gluttony, laziness, ingratitude all lie heavily upon us cutting us off from him. 'God's eyes are too holy to behold evil' (Habakkuk 1:13) so how can God look into my soul and be my friend? The answer is he can and he will have fellowship with me but that fellowship has come at a price and that price was paid in the loving initiative of the Cross.

When people outside Christian circles debate with us about the Cross we find common ground in a perception that the world needs putting right by forgiveness. To get beyond the stumbling block of divine love willing suffering requires a vision of God with loving sameness to yet holy difference from us. Attaining such a vision can follow scrutiny of Christian basics where there is readiness to take seriously what God might have said of God, history and the future through scripture and the community of faith. Faith seeming to contradict logic brings an invitation to seek the understanding beyond reason the Holy Spirit supplies seekers. Without the Spirit the Cross of Jesus would not be on the daily agenda of so many 2000 years on.

12
Guilt

Gilbert Chesterton was one of the brightest Christian minds of the last century. When a newspaper asked several writers to answer the question 'What is wrong with the world?' Chesterton answered: 'Dear Sirs, I am. Sincerely yours, G. K. Chesterton'. The short statement - I am a sinner - cuts through to the bottom line of human existence. Sinners sin and in consequence things fall apart in their lives and relationships and in the world as a whole. In his smart riposte on what is wrong with the world Chesterton begs questions about sin, guilt and forgiveness. If human beings have messed up the world how can they help get it right again? Over my years as a priest people have come to me haunted by guilt about what they have done knowing the Church can deal with that guilt. By the time they reach me most have accepted blame for their action and intend to leave the past behind. It is a joy to see clouds of guilt lifted as they voice repentance and new energy for putting themselves and their world right emerges through assurance bringing the Bible alive to them. Sometimes though they return with the same complaint, back under the clouds, to be gently rebuked for lack of faith in what Jesus did for them on the Cross. We receive forgiveness and sometimes go on to doubt it because it seems too good to be true. When God says he forgives those sorry for their sins, he forgives. This is counter to the perception that guilt is a punishment we justly carry for wrongdoing. 'That sorrow, even for sin, may be overmuch. That overmuch sorrow swallows one up' (Richard Baxter). When accepted deep down the forgiveness of sins breaks this grip. It is a spiritual resurrection wonderful to experience as well as to be witness to.

Guilt is linked to failure which sometimes is imagined or exaggerated. I think of carers whose loved ones have died speaking of their regrets at not helping them seek treatment sooner or not being there at the moment of death. People feel guilty about inheriting their loved one's wealth as a consequence of their death. In a more searching way guilt follows perceived breaking of the moral law. To live aware of such a law we regularly transgress is so difficult for some that they project blame upon Christians and others for upholding this law which seems cause of their guilt. By contrast Christians relate to moral standards with humility and hope knowing a higher power to be at work than their conscience. When I fail to tell the whole truth, join in a conversation judging others or harbour thoughts of superiority the inner voice of my conscience starts to whisper and eventually shout. Eventually - and one measure of holiness is the length of time taken - guilt of wrongdoing is owned, I repent, seek forgiveness from God for my sin, resolve, and then act to put things right with others. In this process I am both accepting I am a sinner and yet that I am accepted by the holy love of God desirous to cleanse me of my sins as part of a lifelong process. The wonder of this process is the removal of guilt. To remain concerned about the consequences of my sin to God, myself and others is distinct from continuing to feel guilty about sins forgiven. That is wrong in a Christian perspective because it implies disbelief in what was achieved once and for all by Jesus on the Cross. You cannot accept forgiveness for your sins and act as if they still weigh upon you and not Jesus because he died to carry the sins we bring to him. To do so is to act with ingratitude towards the grace of God.

Despite a popular distortion, Christianity is guilt-ridding not guilt-ridden. Of course it is a very humiliating matter, facing up to your sins. Guilt-ridding comes at a cost to our pride. We have to admit we have sinned and ask for forgiveness before we can get rid of our sins. People do not like it and this may be why Christian opposition to immoral behaviour is sometimes resented. Some will always want to indulge themselves irrespective of the consequences to themselves and to society. However there is a widespread perception of self-righteousness about Christians as if they are always doing people down compared to themselves, rubbing into others rather than themselves that they are sinners. It is one thing to write as Chesterton did implying he is a sinner and another to write, as I am doing here, of other people indeed of all people being sinners. Although that is what scripture says (Romans 3:23) we need help in facing up to the truth of it, the revelation provided in Christ of God's love for sinners out of which he offers forgiveness to the repentant. The Founder of Christianity died and rose to bring us the forgiveness of sins which is the antidote to guilt. Christianity is primarily about grace, acceptance and love - not condemnation and guilt - and once we meet Jesus we recognise that even if his followers can at times signal otherwise.

This controversy surrounding Christianity and guilt runs the risk of blinding us to the healthy role of guilt I described in my own experience of repentance. If our consciences are informed, by knowledge of the bible and the consensus of moral teaching deriving from it, they will alert us when we do wrong and encourage us to repent. Being burdened by wrongdoing without any resolve to correct it is a guilt trip in the worst sense. This contrast is described by St Paul in his second letter to Corinth: 'I rejoice, not because you were grieved, but because your grief led to repentance; for you felt a godly grief, so that you were not harmed in any way by us. For godly grief produces a repentance that leads to salvation and brings no regret, but worldly grief produces death' (2 Corinthians 7:9-10). Paul Coughlin provides a helpful commentary on godly sorrow for sin: 'Compare the misery from false guilt to the beneficial nature of healthy guilt, or what Christian counsellors sometimes call godly sorrow. Victor Frankl, founder of Logotherapy, one of the most muscular and real-world attempts to make sense of life's suffering (Frankl was a Holocaust survivor), praised guilt as one of three components that make the case for what he called "Tragic Optimism." He said that the tragic triad of life are pain, guilt and death. Yet if handled properly, they can spur a person toward abiding meaning and purpose in life. Through guilt, he wrote, people have the potential to change for the better. Healthy guilt is a gatekeeper and boundary-maker. It helps us discover where we shouldn't go in life, what we shouldn't do. And it helps us make amends when we do cause others pain and related hardships. Guilt helps us find our way back toward what's right and repair the torn portions of our lives.' (36)

No one on earth escapes the tragic triad of pain or death or guilt so often interwoven but the way we deal with them can be transformative. Guilt has a past reference. Its overcoming by forgiveness turns a page in your life bestowing a new start. God who brings life out of nothing in creation and the risen Jesus from an empty tomb is able to recreate believers and 'by the power at work within us is able to accomplish abundantly far more than all we can ask or imagine' (Ephesians 3:20). If Christianity is accused of being focused on guilt it is in the same way that we focus on dealing with a blockage to remedy a malfunctioning flow. In St John's Gospel Chapter 7 we read 'Let anyone who is thirsty come to me, and let the one who believes in me drink. Out of the believer's heart shall flow rivers of living water. Now Jesus said this about the Spirit, which believers in him were to receive' (John 7:38-39). Coming to Jesus for the forgiveness of sins breaks the grip of past failings over us. As this passage implies, dealing with guilt by coming to the Cross opens up a spiritual resurrection with fresh momentum in life from the dynamic of the Holy Spirit. This renews our future orientation of life: 'And all of us, with unveiled faces, seeing the glory of the Lord as though reflected in a mirror, are being transformed into the same image from one degree of glory to another; for this comes from the Lord, the Spirit' (2 Corinthians 3:18). Guilt put aside we 'look now forwards, and let the backwards be' (The Cloud of Unknowing)

13
Hell

The doctrine of hell upheld in the Athanasian Creed is contested on account of difficulties in understanding how God could send people there as well as misuse of the fear of hell by the Church through history. There is also linguistic confusion with the reference to Christ's 'descending into hell' in the Apostles' Creed where the old English word 'hell' has a different meaning. Nevertheless belief in hell as a place of eternal punishment for unrepentant sinners is part of the faith of the church through the ages. The doctrine is well founded in scripture, revealed by God in Jesus Christ and seen as the logical consequence of ultimate adherence by the soul to its own will in rejection of the will of God. Fear of hell like fear of God is controversial but it is grounded in 'the Love that moves the stars and the sun' to use Dante's phrase even if his imagery of hell, like that of scripture, begs reconsideration. At the centre of that holy fear is the watchfulness over our lives that Jesus Christ calls us to: 'If your hand causes you to stumble, cut it off; it is better for you to enter life maimed than to have two hands and to go to hell, to the unquenchable fire where 'Their worm does not die; And the fire is not quenched' (Mark 9:43-48).

The Creed of Saint Athanasius ranks with the Apostles' and Nicene Creeds as definitive of Christian Faith though it is more rarely used in worship. Its section on Christ's hoped for return to judge the living and the dead ends: 'at whose coming all men shall rise again with their bodies: and shall give account for their own works. And they that have done good shall go into life everlasting: and they that have done evil into everlasting fire' (37). Hell as that place of torment is not mentioned by name in this Creed though, confusingly, it is found in the Apostles' Creed in the sense of the realm of the dead as a whole: '[Christ] descended into hell' (38). 'Hell' here is linked to the Anglo-Saxon behelian, 'to hide', implying a dark hidden place linked to the Creed's Latin 'inferus' or place below. The Athanasian Creed speaks of the hell of condemnation, 'infernus' or place of fire linked to punishment after death. Whilst the hell of the Apostles' Creed links to the Hebrew 'Sheol' used for the place of the dead, the sentence in the Athanasian Creed reflects 'Gehenna' or place of torment for the wicked which had visual association in Christ's day with the ever burning rubbish dump outside the walls of Jerusalem.

Disbelief in hell is associated with widespread disbelief in God and the immortality of the soul. Among Christians the former is in question among some as is the last, seen as an import into Christianity from Greek thought. Some think there is no life beyond death save that which the immortal Christ shares with believers so that death for unbelievers is extinction. 2 Thessalonians 2:8 supports annihilation rather than eternal punishment for those who refuse God's salvation: 'And then the lawless one will be revealed, whom the Lord Jesus will destroy with the breath of his mouth, annihilating him by the manifestation of his coming'. Conversely, when the immortality of the soul is accepted, the question of its eternal place in relation to God is paramount. Can a human being not cleansed or redeemed by God be with him? God is holy and can have no fellowship with what is unholy (Revelation 21:27). Uncleansed souls would need separating from God in their eternal state which is one understanding of the necessity of hell.

Returning to internal Christian controversy about the doctrine, there is just concern about past and present use of it to frighten people into joining the Church. Forms of evangelisation that fail to validate people as loved by God are rightly suspect. At the same time misuse of teaching about hell is no excuse for dismissing its reality since the Founder of Christianity taught its existence in parables warning religious leaders against hypocrisy and rich people against indifference to the poor. 'Just as the weeds are collected and burned up with fire, so will it be at the end of the age. The Son of Man will send his angels, and they will collect out of his kingdom all causes of sin and all evildoers, and they will throw them into the furnace of fire, where there will be weeping and gnashing of teeth. Then the righteous will shine like the sun in the kingdom of their Father' (Matthew 13:40-43). In Matthew Chapter 25 Jesus speaks of the separation at the end time of 'sheep' and 'goats', of those inheriting God's kingdom as against those departing to destruction. In the story of the rich man and Lazarus, the poor man, Christ paints a picture of a great gulf fixed between heaven and hell. Would Jesus have taught this, and spoken so much of the urgent need to choose the right path, by repenting and believing in God, if that were unnecessary?

How can a loving God revealed in Jesus Christ condemn people to hell? There is a continual emphasis in scripture on two courses for human beings. The way of righteousness leads to heavenly glory. The way of selfishness leads to eternal darkness. Even if wickedness sometimes appears to triumph on earth, the doctrines of heaven and hell affirm God will ultimately have his way - with us or without us. Second century writer Justin taught that if hell does not exist 'either there is no God, or if there is, he does not concern himself with men, and virtue and vice have no meaning'.

Concern of God for humanity is at the heart of the Christian revelation which is Christ's death out of love for the world. This affirms even people determined to go their own way are respected by God whose love for them is so pure he will not manipulate them away from hell. Those seeing themselves as self-made men and women should be able to worship their perceived creator forever in that darkness. Any discussion about hell leads back to the whole purpose of this life in relation to the world to come, especially whether there *is* a world to come and how you best prepare for it. Cardinal Newman wrote 150 years ago that 'life is short, death is certain and the world to come is everlasting'. In the world today life is not so short thanks to improved nutrition and medicine. The certainty of death is edited out of public life or presented as remote from us as individuals. Is there a *greater* certainty than death? Is there someone who has overcome the power of death and has the capacity to offer life without end? These are questions Christians will raise when people want to dismiss hell with any thought of eternal destiny for humankind.

In his novel 'The Great Divorce' CS Lewis portrays a grim place where it rains continuously and the offer of an extraordinary excursion up through the rain clouds to a beautiful country above. As people travel their bodies become ghost-like and on arrival they find a world unyieldingly solid unlike themselves with shining figures they once knew on earth who encourage them to make their own way to this land through repentance and seeking God. Despite this experience of solid joys almost all the ghost-like people make their excuses choosing return to their shadowy existence below. What is striking about the story is the divorce between heaven and hell and how thin yet plausible are the excuses made for preferring the latter.

When people asked Jesus if many would be saved his answer was: 'Enter through the narrow gate; for the gate is wide and the road is easy that leads to destruction, and there are many who take it. For the gate is narrow and the road is hard that leads to life, and there are few who find it' (Matthew 7:13-14) As Lewis presents in his novel, no one drifts into the kingdom of heaven. Contrary to popular imagination entry is not automatic. It is possible though to drift into hell (39).

Belief in hell is a corollary to the active seeking of God in his holiness at the heart of Christianity. Fear of hell is linked to fear of slipping away from our Saviour who, like a 'life preserver, has cast himself into the troubled waters of human existence so that all who keep hold of him are saved from eternal separation from God. 'Indeed, God did not send the Son into the world to condemn the world, but in order that the world might be saved through him. Those who believe in him are not condemned; but those who do not believe are condemned already, because they have not believed in the name of the only Son of God (John 3:17-18).

14
Judgement

'Jesus Christ will come to judge the living and the dead' says the Apostles' Creed so that God who is truth sees the ultimate triumph of truth over falsehood (40). It is Christian faith that we live in hope of that moment of judgement to come individually and generally. The doctrine of judgement extrapolates from those of creation and redemption linked to the person of Jesus Christ seen as having won the right to assert the definitive triumph of good over evil and truth over falsehood. 'Nothing is covered up that will not be uncovered, and nothing secret that will not become known' (Luke 12:2). Christ himself demonstrated such unveiling of truth throughout his earthly ministry and encouraged people to face up to their shortfalls offering forgiveness and healing. 'You will know the truth, and the truth will make you free' (John 8:32). Facing the truth is a great human problem addressed by Christianity. That we humans find it hard to own our shortcomings is linked to bad experiences in our past when we have been treated harshly for our sins. This makes the idea of forgiveness novel and the idea of ultimate judgement unthinkable. Encountering the love of God in Jesus Christ through word and sacrament, prayer and Christian fellowship brings conviction of our acceptance and the forgiveness of our sins. This in turn removes fear of facing God at death or at the final judgement, whilst keeping us alert to the danger of presumption, since 'there is no condemnation for those who are in Christ Jesus' (Romans 8:1).

Truth-telling has implications both for individuals and society. Speaking on the BBC about the social responsibility of global media agencies Alan Rusbridger drew this analogy. 'Just as a society can't function without clean water it cannot function without clean information' (41). In the wake of Donald Trump's Presidency and removal from Twitter, Rusbridger was addressing the literal cost of truth telling such as researching items in the public domain to check their veracity. There is a balancing act on social media between freedom of speech and information against dangers from unfiltered speech and misinformation. Are social media organisations platforms for anyone to speak or, as indicated by the removal of a US President from one, a publishing agency with responsibility concerning the truth content of what they publish? If it is the latter there will be costs involved to them which would affect their working through the need to recoup these. Living in truth as a society is inseparable from taking responsibility for unveiling falsehoods. Like the need to clean up water before it goes through house pipes there is a need to cleanse society from untruths that cause dysfunction. Christians, though like others deceived at times by the media, have a special investment in truth-telling as they witness to God who is truth. Belief in the return of Christ to judge the world is foundational to conviction of the greatness and ultimate triumph of truth and justice.

In Dostoyevsky's classic novel 'The Brothers Karamazov' two brothers argue about the evil in the world and whether there is ultimate justice. The debate comes to a point where one of the brothers says he is so outraged by the suffering of children that, given a place in heaven, he would refuse it in protest (42). The other brother replies by pointing to the suffering of Jesus. Does God expect anything of us that he has not been through himself? The judge of the world is not aloof. In Christian faith it is through Jesus that God will provide the ultimate righting of wrongs. God has invested in the human race. One day he will get a return on that investment. We get a glimpse of the judgement and fulfilment of all things in the book of Revelation 11:15 where we read 'the kingdom of the world has become the kingdom of our Lord and of his Christ, and he shall reign forever and ever'. To believe in the judgement of the living and the dead is to believe in the coming of this kingdom and the trumping of the rule of evil and God's triumph over injustice in this world at Christ's return. Jesus Christ who came, died and rose has yet to complete his great and saving purpose. This purpose is described in the letter to the Ephesians as the seeking of a bride by a heavenly bridegroom. To the eye of Christian faith the whole of human and cosmic history has this purpose: to prepare a holy people for God's possession. The church is this, a bride being prepared 'without spot or wrinkle' (Ephesians 5:27) for a heavenly destiny when her Lord comes again. In this eternal perspective all the sufferings of this world endured in faith will 'work for good for those who love the Lord' (Romans 8:28). 'Christ has died! Christ is risen! Christ will come again!' This is Christian faith and it brings an assurance that evil's triumph in this world will be short lived. God will turn the wrath of man to his praise by the building up of the body of Christ as 'a people for his own possession' (1 Peter 2:9).

How can judgement be possible? Can there really be a final catalogue of wrongdoing? Surely there can, Christian faith replies. As surely as a computer memory contains a million records, the memory of God is established. To him all hearts are open and all desires known. By his sharing in our nature and his boundless compassion Jesus Christ is well appointed to judge the living and the dead. Did he not welcome and put the best slant on thieves and prostitutes, always ready to treat people as better than they were? Christian tradition distinguishes an individual judgement at the moment of death and a general judgement which completes God's righteous task at the Lord's return. After death scripture speaks of two ultimate destinies, heaven and hell, although there is a qualification that no one dying with unrepented sin can face the Lord without cleansing since 'no unclean thing shall enter' his presence (Revelation 21:27). This is the origin of the doctrine of purgatory which in its plain sense of the need for the faithful departed to be purged or cleansed of residual sin to come close to God is hard to counter. The other historical understanding of purgatory as a place where the closeness to God of the departed can be engineered or even bought by appropriate religious services or exercises was rightly opposed at the reformation.

Our minds argue against judgement because they think they know best. This is the case at times even for believers in God. Though many unbelievers would see truth in relation to the common good its objectivity is naturally in question and the idea of giving account for all their thoughts and actions to God is alien to their sense of autonomy. So is the implied threat of judgment so often captured graphically in medieval art. How might we depict judgment today? Maybe in a more intimate fashion, looking God, who is truth, in the face trusting in his loving capacity to forgive. When we look into the eyes of Christ at his return there will be pain, but it should be seen as an 'if the cap fits wear it' sort of pain. Owning and confessing falsehood is our choice. Our wrong actions are an affront to God but he has given us a remedy. As the video of my life is prepared for showing on judgement day Christ has power to edit out the unacceptable points if I give them to him by repenting of them. Mercy triumphs over judgement when we allow Christ a place in our hearts. Scripture assures us there is no condemnation for those who welcome Christ's indwelling. God looks on those in Christ with the same love with which he looks upon his Son. Judgement has in a profound sense been passed already for those who have accepted God's judgement on their lives. To accept one's sinfulness and inadequacy is therefore in Christian tradition a pathway to joy. Such acceptance springs from a vision of God given in Jesus Christ, a God more concerned to give us what we need than to give us what we deserve. To believe in Jesus Christ 'who will come to judge the living and the dead' is to face the future with an infectious hope. If faith shows you that the whole world is in God's hands so is its future. Christianity provides a deep sense of certainty that falsehood and evil will be seen ultimately as illusory. All will come right in the end because in the end there will be the *grace and truth* of Jesus Christ (John 1:14, 17). Ultimately there will be grace – mercy - for repentant sinners and truth to prevail over all who live and act deluded by falsehood.

15
Loving yourself

Brusher Mills was the last and most celebrated of New Forest snake catchers. He died in 1905. A picture survives of him clutching a haul of adders in each hand. Brusher was something of an eccentric. He had a particular way of winning favour with young ladies furtively dropping an adder near a group of them retreating until they screamed. Then he appeared to rescue them from peril! Christianity can be viewed like that, scaring folk with demands to make them feel inadequate and presenting them the Saviour. Like Brusher's tactics for winning ladies there are forms of evangelisation which do damage to truth, especially the truth about ourselves. To some Christianity looks good in principle as an altruistic movement but harsh in galvanising individuals to a cause built seemingly on self-hatred. The founder of Christianity warned, after all, that 'those who want to save their life will lose it, and those who lose their life for my sake will find it' (Matthew 16:25).

How can Christianity be squared with self-love? Is it not a threat to the positive self-image essential to healthy relationships? Confirmation training in churches I have served encouraged individual confession of sins to prepare for laying on of hands by the Bishop inviting the Holy Spirit. I remember the father of one candidate coming round to see me. 'I'm concerned about what you're doing to David', he said. 'His mum and I are trying to build in him a positive self-image but you are telling him he is a sinner and there is a lot wrong with his life'. This exchange years ago alerted me both to the danger of spiritual abuse in ministry and to the culture clash we have about the nature of sin. It made me determined to do my best to always present Christianity as the validating good news of love it is, affirming people and not putting them down. David's dad did me good service in alerting me to the rightness of self-respect. Just as parents harm their children by doing them down, 'spiritual parents' run the same risk. As children sadly condemn themselves in agreement with judgemental parents so Christianity can be made into the opposite of what it is about - a guilt trip into self-hatred! Guilt is the deep down feeling you have done wrong. This is natural for human beings made with a sense of right and wrong and living with guilty awareness of failing to do right on many occasions. The genius of Christianity is in its guilt-ridding. Jesus Christ came and comes into lives precisely because there is sin there that needs dealing with. The Founder of Christianity died and rose to bring us the forgiveness of sins which is the antidote to guilt. He comes to turn self-hatred into self-love and ultimately self-forgetfulness.

What then did Christ mean saying 'those who lose their life for my sake will find it'? Where is self-respect in that saying? The verse is part of a section of Matthew's Gospel encouraging wholehearted following of God whilst being blunt that the cost of this may be no less for disciples than for their Master. The previous verse mentions crucifixion even as a risk to his followers. 'Jesus told his disciples, "If any want to become my followers, let them deny themselves and take up their cross and follow me' (Matthew 16:24). Stories of Christian martyrs from the book of Acts onward present absorption with the love of God in Jesus Christ that willingly leaves self behind. The first recorded martyr is Stephen whose excitement at his stoning to death links less to self-hatred than to his focus totally away from self. 'They became enraged and ground their teeth at Stephen. But filled with the Holy Spirit, he gazed into heaven and saw the glory of God and Jesus standing at the right hand of God. "Look," he said, "I see the heavens opened and the Son of Man standing at the right hand of God!" But they covered their ears, and with a loud shout all rushed together against him... Then they dragged him out of the city and... while they were stoning Stephen, he prayed, "Lord Jesus, receive my spirit." Then he knelt down and cried out in a loud voice, "Lord, do not hold this sin against them." When he had said this, he died' (Acts 7:54-58a, 59-60). How could such love towards your murderers exclude anyone, least of all yourself? This description of his death shows Stephen's valuing of himself in his final words of entrustment to the One he loved. Earlier in the Acts account we read how heavenly love enfolded him when 'all who sat in the council looked intently at him, and they saw that his face was like the face of an angel' (Acts 6:15). Stephen knew himself, possessed himself and so was able to face the challenge to give himself. If his attention had been more self-indulgent that gift would not have been possible but something had happened in his life to take his attention away from self making 'Stephen, full of grace and power' (Acts 6:8)

'Know yourself, love yourself, forget yourself' are three headings used in traditional Christian retreats placing self-love central. That love is distinct from the hatred for sin self-knowledge invites and the self-forgetfulness attained as attention is drawn away from self to God. This repetitive process is described in the purgative, illuminative and unitive stages identified by St John of the Cross in which seeking the Holy Spirit is the clue to losing sin, seeing more of God and, being attracted to him, seeing more sin for purging. Those who believe Christianity to be an enemy of self-love miss how self-love gets bound to desire for holiness once God comes on the scene bringing his invitation to self knowledge and self forgetfulness. That is why Christians see knowledge of God and knowledge of self as in parallel with neither fully attainable in this life. That they can be put in parallel affirms the sameness of our being and God's, for example, that we can be in a loving personal relationship. Holiness by contrast is a quality more linked to God's difference from us and sin, from the human end, a reminder of our difference from God. God is also no being just like us but the ground of our being. As we become aware of his love and holiness enfolding us this affirms self-love - we are so valued - and challenges it through the impact of holiness upon us.

Christ's challenge to take up his cross is linked to the forward movement of following him as a disciple 'laying aside every weight and the sin that clings so closely' (Hebrews 12:1) as we run the race of the faith. Of course it is a very serious matter, facing up to your sins, and altogether humiliating. Guilt-ridding can only occur at a cost to our pride. We have to admit our sins and to ask for forgiveness before we can get rid of them. People do not like it since Christian opposition to immoral behaviour is often resented. Some will always want to indulge themselves irrespective of consequences to themselves and to society. If the church is said to have a guilt problem the world has a lack of guilt problem! C S Lewis described his own guilty feelings as being like toothache and how he delayed dealing with them just like delaying attending to a bad tooth out of fear of the dentist. People refuse to face up to their sins and do something about them maybe because, unlike Lewis, they do not have a dentist, so to speak. They do not know there is a provision in Jesus for overcoming the power of sin. People who will not face their sins can end up marking time on their spiritual journey. They complain about Christianity because it offers them a grace they have come to live without. It 'rattles their cage' maybe!

Christianity is a holiness movement that will not rest with being held back by sin. It is always going to challenge where we are at, whether we have yet to start the journey of faith or are actually on that journey. Jesus came to save the world and not to judge it but people have to give him the chance to save them by opening up their hearts for him to cleanse. God always treats us as better than we are when we will allow him access to our lives. God's love once recognised builds self-love setting it in a grander scheme of the community of believers and the transforming impact of self-forgetfulness upon the world. In the bible based vision of the Trinity each person within God loses themselves in the affirmation of the other, the Father for the Son, the Son for the Father with the go-between Holy Spirit. Self-love was there before the world was made within Godself and it will be expanded in self-forgetfulness, when the universe has run its course within the communion of saints.

16
Marian controversy

If there is a controversial figure in Christianity beyond Jesus himself it is his mother Mary. I have found people who love her more than Jesus, people hostile to her as a distraction to faith and people who cannot understand the fuss about her. Mary rides on controversies about authority in the church, the nature of prayer and the experience of the supernatural. Shedding light on her is about opening closed doors between Catholic and Protestant and windows to the breeze of the Spirit of truth linked to Mary.

Sally came to see me because she could only pray to Mary. She knew as a Christian she should pray to Jesus but guilt about her son's marriage breakdown prevented her. She felt Jesus was angry with her so it was better to go to Mary. In ministering to her I discovered something of a culture alien to me in which the saints rather than Jesus are go-betweens with God. Meeting Sally confirmed prejudice instilled in me about Catholics being on the wrong track about Mary as I was asked to put this Catholic right. The task was helped by Sally's eagerness to seek forgiveness for wrong things in her life and her recognition that Jesus, not Mary, could accomplish this which he did as she opened up to the Holy Spirit. In talking to her I was careful to commend ongoing Marian devotion so she would see Mary as her prayer minister above as she had just been helped by my earthly prayers.

Jim, by contrast, discovered heaven saying the 'Hail Mary'. Of Protestant background he had been put off Mary, joking how she was taught to him as just another dead Roman Catholic! Bereavement got Jim thinking about the departed. Worshipping in an Anglocatholic Church using the 'Hail Mary' prayer got him questioning teaching about the Christian departed being absent from us as asleep. The dead, even if they had accepted Jesus, were not to be seen as present to us but in a separate realm. To talk to saints made you guilty of the spiritualism condemned in the bible. Led eventually to join in the 'Hail Mary' it dawned on Jim that Mary - heaven - was at his level and to be engaged with since all believers are 'raised up with Christ and seated with him in the heavenly places' (Ephesians 2:6). He felt the closeness of Mary seated beside him on Christ's throne, privilege of believers, and it was now natural for him to invoke her prayers.

Christian controversy about Mary remains despite the scripture promise that 'all generations will call [Mary] blessed' Luke 1:48. It is biblical to magnify Mary because God himself honoured her in making her Mother of his only Son Jesus Christ sent to be the Saviour of the world. Week by week Christians honour Mary as they profess that 'the only Son of God... for us and for our salvation... came down from heaven, was incarnate from the Holy Spirit and the Virgin Mary and was made man' (Nicene Creed). Salvation came into the world through the unique partnership of God and Mary. Though the choice of Mary is God's, and her cooperation is inspired by God, it remains an astonishing truth that without that cooperation the cosmos would not be redeemed. The idea magnifying Mary diminishes Jesus seems strange, at least in principle. There is no competition between them in the Gospels where Mary repeatedly points to her Son as Saviour. She did this silently standing by his Cross where out of love for her Jesus gave Mary to John's care: '"Woman, here is your son." Then he said to the disciple, "Here is your mother."' (John 19:26-27). Many like Jim discover that gift as one going beyond John to all believers. As the opening lines of an Anglican hymn state: 'Shall we not love thee, Mother dear, whom Jesus loved so well?' (43)

Controversy around Mary links to controversy about authority in the Church. At the Reformation a section of Christendom prided itself in testing doctrine and devotion against the plain sense of scripture. St Paul, who has no mention of Mary in his writings, is a key influence. Roman Catholic doctrine, formulated from scripture and tradition by the consensus of bishops headed by the Pope, is seen by

Protestants as weak in its biblical basis. The doctrines of Mary's conception without sin, perpetual virginity and bodily assumption are rejected in consequence by many although none are contradicted by scripture. The 2005 Anglican-RC statement on Mary says 'we agree that doctrines and devotions which are contrary to Scripture cannot be said to be revealed by God nor to be the teaching of the Church' (44). This agreement captures the spirit of the Second Vatican Council (1962-5) whose Constitution on the Church states: 'This Synod earnestly exhorts theologians and preachers of the divine word that in treating of the unique dignity of the Mother of God, they carefully and equally avoid the falsity of exaggeration on the one hand, and the excess of narrow-mindedness on the other... Pursuing the study of the sacred scripture, the holy Fathers, the doctors and liturgies of the church, and under the guidance of the church's teaching authority, let them rightly explain the offices [roles] and privileges of the Blessed Virgin which are always related to Christ, the source of all truth, sanctity and piety' (45)

Over the years since Vatican II the importance of Mary as model Christian has been more recognised across denominations. In her 'Yes' to God given to the Archangel Gabriel and confirmed in the hardships she bore, Mary models unselfish obedience. Simeon prophesied her heart would be 'pierced with a sword' (Luke 2:35) and we see this fulfilled in Mary's presence at the foot of the Cross, obediently following her Son in his sufferings. She is model Christian, one with us, exemplifying obedience to God in sorrow and in joy. At Cana she gives advice to the servants to be taken more widely: 'Do whatever [Jesus] tells you!' (John 2:5). Art over the centuries has attempted to capture the radiance of Mary as God-bearer. As the Archangel promised, 'The Holy Spirit will come upon you, and the power of the Most High will overshadow you; therefore the child to be born will be holy; he will be called Son of God' (Luke 1:35). It is a widely accepted view, as expressed in the Church of England Prayer Book, that the Holy Spirit kept Mary 'a pure Virgin' freeing her from sin to be a fitting instrument of the Saviour's birth. Through the Charismatic Movement Mary's prayerful presence in Acts 1:14 associated with Pentecost has made her an icon of the Spirit-filled Christian life. The feast of Mary's passing into heaven (15 August) is now kept across traditions even if its biblical base in the prophecy of John remains questioned: 'A great portent appeared in heaven: a woman clothed with the sun, with the moon under her feet, and on her head a crown of twelve stars' (Revelation 12:1).

As a heavy smoker I came to see a contradiction between filling my body with smoke whilst claiming to be filled with the Spirit. I found a devotion to Spirit-filled Mary kindled on pilgrimage to her Shrine at Walsingham in Norfolk. I knelt down in the Holy House sensing no one on earth or in heaven prayed for me as effectively as the Mother of Jesus. She knew what Jesus wanted. I asked to be freed from smoking thirty cigarettes a day and I was. From that day Mary's intercession came real to me though I hold back from the traditionalist devotion to Mary as Mediatrix. 'There is one mediator between God and humankind, Christ Jesus' (1 Timothy 2:5). Jesus made clear all Christians gain a share in that unique mediation so that 'anything we ask in his name he will give to us' (John 14:13). The only qualification we have as his intercessors is close abiding in him, an unquestionable quality of Mary, and expectation of the supernatural power of God. Such expectation has been much associated with apparitions of the Virgin Mary over the centuries. These have come with prophetic messages calling for repentance and deeper trust in God in the face of hardship and persecution or of apathy and indifference towards God. Appearances to simple folk, often very poor as at Lourdes and Fatima, resonate with Mary's own calling at Nazareth. Miracles associated with these apparitions amplify Mary's thanksgiving to God recorded in her Magnificat: 'the Mighty One has done great things for me, and holy is his name' (Luke 1:49).

Welcoming light on Marian controversy is helped by firsthand experience of the power of her prayer. Otherwise divisions about Mary can seem of little relevance reflecting institutional pride more than the humility Mary commends. If trust, obedience and Holy Spirit empowerment flow from

Mary's purity our own distrust, disobedience and spiritual apathy flow from our impurity. It is good to capture her warmth, joy and radiance which shine into all the questioning about her.

JOHN TWISLETON

17
Ordination of women

'Can Jesus be preached in the whole world without ecclesiasticism? asked Friedrich Naumann, an exponent of charismatic religion [a century ago], 'can molten gold be carried from place to place in anything but crucibles of iron and steel?' This image of the Church as a crucible transporting molten gold captures its secondary role in Christianity alongside its service of love, truth and empowerment in Jesus Christ (46). Charismatics like Naumann are in that flow of the Spirit alongside feminists whose courageous action has challenged male dominance within the institutional crucible in recent years. The crucible analogy captures something of why Christianity is content to retain antiquated institutions as its main concern is not on the carrier but on its effective instrumentality. Crucibles are of not so sightly, tough iron and when in use our eyes are drawn not to them but to the splendour of what they carry. When they crack, though, they prove useless. This analogy may help explain the best aspect of resistance to the ordination of women in the greatest body of the Church, Roman Catholic and Orthodox, who see the episcopate as a focus of unity. Seeing the dispute about ordaining women outside the Roman Catholic Church, Pope John Paul II seems to have been driven to settle the question for Roman Catholics with near infallible use of the Petrine ministry: 'In order that all doubt may be removed regarding a matter of great importance, a matter which pertains to the Church's divine constitution itself, in virtue of my ministry of confirming the brethren (cf. Lk 22:32) I declare that the Church has no authority whatsoever to confer priestly ordination on women and that this judgment is to be definitively held by all the Church's faithful' (47).

Even if Roman Catholic authority has closed debate on the ordination of women, and there is little debate within Orthodoxy, other Christian traditions have been ordaining women for over a century. The exclusion of women from leadership has been seen as an unjust violation of human dignity, weakening mission through loss of women's gifts being exercised in oversight. Since the Reformation, part of Christian tradition has raised questions about whether ordination is essential to Christianity. Is it of the 'esse' of the Church, essential, or only of the 'bene esse', beneficial as leadership is to any organisation? The question of authorising female ordination is complicated by such questions about the constitution of the Church, authority and leadership within it. When Pope John Paul II said the matter 'pertains to the Church's divine constitution' he implied it was not for human agency, even a Pope bearing Christ's commission to St Peter, to change the divine Saviour's choice of male apostles as the foundation of his Church. Other traditions who dispute papal authority also dispute the divinity of the Church and the role of sacred ministers in representing Christ, for which the ordination of women is a symbolic dislocation in the traditional sacramental understanding. The ordination of women seems less of a difficulty when this understanding of the priest as 'alter Christus' (the other Christ) is rejected. The New Testament speaks of Christ's priesthood and that of the Church as a whole with fewer texts speaking of the priestly nature of the ordained ministry. It also speaks of the equality of men and women in Christ, as in Galatians 3:28, 'There is no longer Jew or Greek... male or female; for all of you are one in Christ Jesus'. Some from the Reformed tradition, so-called 'conservative Evangelicals', balance this scriptural teaching of equality between the sexes with a principle of sexual differentiation. The headship principle based on Genesis Chapters 1-2 is presupposed by most of the Bible and spelled out in Ephesians 5:22-25, 'Be subject to one another out of reverence for Christ. Wives, be subject to your husbands as you are to the Lord. For the husband is the head of the wife just as Christ is the head of the church, the body of which he is the Saviour. Just as the church is subject to Christ, so also wives ought to be, in everything, to their husbands. Husbands, love your wives, just as Christ loved the church and gave himself up for her'. Many scripture commentators though see this sort of headship as something time bound which is justly to be reinterpreted in our day.

Writing as a man about the ordination of women risks being patronising. The matter requires elucidation, so Christian practice to date is seen as less discriminatory than it looks, and yet the look and feel of the matter is affected by the gender of the writer and reader so I apologise in advance of speaking more personally. I have first hand experience of the Anglican debate in both England and the Caribbean in consequence of which I am impatient about reduction of the matter to being a simple matter of justice. It is wrong to change the Church simply because of contemporary beliefs just as it is wrong to dismiss the callings many women have felt towards ordained ministry. To accept the ordination of women in the name of making the Christian good news accessible is only misguided if it compromises foundational Christian truth, the 'esse' or essentials of the Church about which the jury remains out ecumenically. With many Provinces now allowing the ordination of women, seen as a God-send to vocations, the Anglican Church has exercised the right to develop its own orders of ministry as it did at the Reformation, allowing married priests, adapting to circumstances. The progress towards women bishops in the Church of England came in the face of warnings that it would make the goal of visible unity with Rome and the Orthodox 'unreachable' (Cardinal Kasper) on account of the Catholic understanding of bishops as a focus of unity for both people in their dioceses and in relation to other bishops across the Christian world. With women's gifts in leadership exercised at very different levels worldwide the acceptance by some Anglicans of the ordination of women bishops has caused impairment of full communion across Anglicanism. The loss in the ecumenical dimension and the internal divisions associated with the ordination of women have been balanced by the fruitful ministry of many women deacons, priests and bishops among Anglicans and Lutherans in recent years. In elucidating women's ordination I have an eye to the Church universal, and its reluctance to move on this, but also on how God has used women in ministry. Thinking about things is distinct from the reality of things and this reality for many Anglicans is a given even if it is a qualified gift, as expressed in 'The Five Guiding Principles' of 2014: 'The Church of England is fully and unequivocally committed to all orders of ministry being open equally to all, without reference to gender... Since it continues to share the historic episcopate with other Churches... which continue to ordain only men as priests or bishops, the Church of England acknowledges that its own clear decision on ministry and gender is set within a broader process of discernment within... the whole Church of God... Since those within the Church of England who, on grounds of theological conviction, are unable to receive the ministry of women bishops or priests continue to be within the spectrum of teaching and tradition of the Anglican Communion, the Church of England remains committed to enabling them to flourish within its life and structures' (48). In confirming that these Principles need to be read 'one with the other and held in tension, rather than being applied selectively' Church of England Bishops make explicit the tension women's ordination creates within and beyond their membership.

Looking to the molten gold of the love, truth and empowerment of Christ's Spirit it is humbling to see the Church's stewardship of this. It is humiliating for Christians to witness the historic divisions, which do little to commend their cause, shown up in their varied response to righting discrimination against women across the world. For Roman Catholics and Orthodox whatever people think about the ordination of women there is a clear line to be respected albeit, for some, with critical loyalty. For Protestants, save conservative Evangelicals, it seems to be a lesser issue as leadership is key more than ordination. Anglicans fall in between with many women choosing to follow vocations now acceptable to the Church and other individuals keeping under the authority of the church through the ages, effected by judicious ordination of bishops, unable to receive these new ministries. The ordination of women is happening and bringing blessings and challenges across the Christian world. Whether it is to be a phase, like the isolated figure of Deborah among centuries of Israelite judges, or to be a Spirit-led reshaping of the institution of the Church we await the verdict of history.

18
Reasonable faith

'Always be ready to make your defense ('apologia') to anyone who demands from you an accounting for the hope that is in you; yet do it with gentleness and reverence' (1 Peter 3:15-16). In those words the New Testament commends the rationality of Christian faith and so-called apologetics which is not about apologising for faith but issuing a rational defence or 'apologia' when you are challenged about believing. With decreased religious literacy people see 'faith' as loyalty to what is contrary to the facts rather than what goes beyond appearance. To have faith in God is seen less as linked to a rational judgment on the evidence that points to God's existence than to credulity in believing what cannot be true. 'You cannot believe what you cannot see' voices a contradiction since in so much of life we put faith in what is actually invisible to the eye like the electricity that powers so much of modern living. The fundamental of fundamentals when it comes to faith is the conviction that there is more to life than meets the eye even if it requires an imaginative yet reasoned leap to engage with this. As scripture says, 'we look not at what can be seen but at what cannot be seen: for what can be seen is temporary, but what cannot be seen is eternal' (2 Corinthians 4:18). The gift of faith provides us with inner eyes that discern what life is really about. Faith is 'the assurance of things hoped for, the conviction of things not seen' (Hebrews 12:1). Just as we see through a microscope marvels of molecular construction, so the gift of faith helps us engage with a greater marvel. We come from God, we belong to God, we go to God. 'In him we live and move and have our being' (Acts 17:28). By faith we welcome moment by moment the evidence of God the Creator's love in the disarming warmth of a smile, the radiant beauty of light, a parent's loving gaze, the careless joy of a child. To have faith is the greatest privilege in the world enabling us to see beyond what meets the eye.

As a scientist I see faith as a form of wisdom that goes beyond but not against the knowledge accessible to human minds. How can I believe in a God I cannot see? I have made a well weighed decision. That is what faith is – a careful decision to act as if God were there and to be energised by a power outside and beyond oneself. Some things in life cannot be tied down rationally. God is one such thing, and so is much of quantum physics. Priest scientist like myself, the late John Polkinghorne saw similarities in the truth seeking of theologians and quantum physicists. Contrary to popular perception the revelation of truth in physics relies on the subjective imagination of the scientist as well as the objective truth awaiting discovery. Similarly theological pursuit of truth, especially in Christianity, relies on stubborn historical research as well as philosophical speculation. There are analogies such as the elements of surprise in both fields. Superconductivity in metals at low temperatures breaks Ohm's law of electrical resistance as surely as Christ's resurrection breaks the universal law of mortality. The moral in truth seeking is a healthy distrust of the popular axiom that what usually happens is what always happens. Believers though, in holding ultimate reality to be purposive, find common ground with science in the perceived rationality of things. Science by definition excludes the supernatural but cannot deny it or the associated realm of metaphysics we are invited into by Christ's resurrection. Polkinghorne puts his mind to an apologia for this, noting the enigmatic rather than triumphalist tone of the Easter accounts. In any made-up tale the difficulty about recognising Jesus would not have emerged and the remarkable role of women as witnesses would not have served credibility in a constructed tale. He concludes: 'Only an understanding of Jesus that sees in him not only full humanity, but also the fullness of the divine life itself, offers a prospect of meeting adequately the demands made by the New Testament witness to him' (49).

Both faith and reason lead us to God so Christian revelation is partner with and not rival to scientific knowledge, as the witness of scientists of faith makes clear. To have faith is to go beyond and not against reason. As John Donne wrote 'Reason is our soul's left hand, faith his right, by these we reach divinity'. Faith and reason lift us to God and in Jesus God himself reaches down to us revealing himself to both our reason and our faith. A reasonable faith is nothing blind even if it is something that cannot be proved. 'It is the one and the same God who establishes and guarantees the intelligibility and reasonableness of the natural order of things upon which scientists confidently depend, and who reveals himself as the Father of our Lord Jesus Christ. This unity of truth, natural and revealed, is embodied in a living and personal way in Christ, as the Apostle reminds us: 'Truth is in Jesus" (cf Eph 4:21)' (50). In Christianity there is an ongoing struggle to hold the truth of God revealed to faith in tandem with what reason dictates to the intellect. Events like the suffering and resurrection of Christ are scrutinised by historians to this day in contrast to less serious consideration of the historicity of many other religions. To those who see faith as a foolish subscription to what is unseen the Christian response is to point to many things real yet unseen like electricity, and to the historical events basic to Christianity. Contested though they are, these events are central to the formulations of faith known as the Christian Creeds.

At this point it is helpful to clarify use of the word 'faith' beyond personal belief in God as subscription to the doctrine of the Church. Believing is placing confidence in someone (eg God) or accepting the truth of something (like the propositions in the Creed eg the forgiveness of sins). There is in use a subjective aspect of faith ('I know whom I have believed' 2 Timothy 1:12) and an objective aspect ('I received from the Lord what I also handed on to you' (1 Corinthians 11v23, cf 15v3). Subscribing to Christian Faith goes beyond individual belief into ownership of the faith of the church through the ages expressed by scripture, creeds, worship and tested ethical norms. Whereas the Apostles' Creed is said in the singular, linking to baptismal commitment, the Nicene and Athanasian Creeds have a plural form. These emphasise corporate commitment to doctrines formulated over the centuries like the Trinity and two natures of Christ as God and man. Believing then has both a personal and ecclesial (church) aspect so Christian initiation involves formation in the church's faith, the creeds, sacraments, commandments and Lord's prayer known as 'catechesis'. Since the Reformation, which asserted the primacy of personal faith, Christians have divided over the church's role and, linked to that, the role of reason in apologetics. Anglicans take a balanced view here seeing Christ's authority carried forward in Christian tradition on the 'three legged stool' of scripture, tradition and reason but with the last seen as inhabited by the Holy Spirit. The latter qualification makes clear how reasonable faith has an eye to thinking in the wider community whilst keeping loyal to scripture and the consensus of faith granted to the church by the Holy Spirit through the ages. What seems unreasonable about Christianity today might either be its counter cultural nature or a possible opening for the Holy Spirit to develop afresh the way faith is being expressed. This role of grace, or the movement of the Holy Spirit in faith, is captured by St Thomas Aquinas (1225-1274) in his famous definition: 'Believing is an act of the intellect assenting to the divine truth by command of the will moved by God through grace'.

Faith without reason leads to superstition or worse and it is the genius of Christianity that it has ultimately remained open to scrutiny and purification over the passage of the centuries. Reason without faith is equally dangerous as the 20th century showed in the dehumanising regimes of Hitler and Stalin dismissing religion to the detriment of millions. If Christianity is true its truth is about humanity and God and how the latter brings the former in its sinful inadequacy to a right mind. As 'Homo sapiens' we are inclined to seek meaning in our lives, a quest that is well served by religion and by Christianity especially, with its personal and purposive centring upon Jesus Christ. It is the fruits of faith that matter, as scripture makes plain: 'For just as the body without the spirit is dead, so faith without works is also dead' (James 2:26). These works are seen in reasonable faith exercised by believers in helping humanity come into its right mind in pursuit of the common good in this world and the next.

19
Sin

Working recently as a School Chaplain helped me see things in a fresh light. The term 'sinner' can be an insult among young people. When we start the eucharist confessing our sins I explain that when we say we are sinners we are recognising all of us do wrong things sometimes. Elucidating sin is a perilous business because no one speaking of it can be distanced from its pervasive influence. There is one extreme downplaying its nature. The people the world might fear most are those claiming innocence from sin. Another extreme, taking Christ's teaching in Matthew 5:28 literally, sees a lustful thought as the end of the road with God. I remember a friend at university convinced that as he could not stop the thoughts he might as well act on them and have sexual intercourse with his girl friend. It was great to meet him years later back in church attendance, a happily married man. The association of sex with sin impacts the understanding of both. I recall preaching an altar call in the Caribbean one Good Friday in a church packed with people of all ages. My words were an invitation to find cleansing from sin by coming to Confession. After my message the parish priest chose to remind the young men that what the preacher said did not just apply to young women getting pregnant out of marriage but to young men getting them so. No men came forward to confession that day!

'Sin is any action or habit which prevents or delays the progress of the soul to perfection, of the danger of which the soul is or ought to be conscious' wrote Anglican bishop and moral theologian Kenneth Kirk. I see my sins as delaying my progress towards what I am meant to be. They hamper my forward progress so that my favourite text on sin is the invitation to 'lay aside every weight and the sin that clings so closely, and run with perseverance the race that is set before us looking to Jesus the pioneer and perfecter of our faith (Hebrews 12:1-2). Over the years the Holy Spirit has shown me more of what clings to me, holding me back in my forward journey, so those bonds can be broken by Jesus who endured the cross to do that for us. It might be lustful thoughts, yes, in youth but it is more likely to be compassion fatigue in the elderly housebound faced day to day with tragic news on television. For many the sins that trip us up include ingratitude, distrust of God, impatience and jealousy of other people's blessings alongside wrong thoughts, words and deeds and omissions. The sense of sin is linked to sensing God and where he wants to take us to be part of building, 'a kingdom of truth and life, a kingdom of holiness and grace, a kingdom of justice, love and peace' (51)

The word 'sin' in Hebrew and Greek is an archery term for 'missing the mark'. This helps us understand our sin as a shortfall in love towards God, neighbour and self. Inasmuch as God commands us to love, sin is disobedient dragging of gifts and energies back from where they should head. Human beings are not sinners because they sin, they sin because they are sinners. Until quite recently the story of Adam and Eve in Genesis was taken literally as the history of how the first man and women got driven from paradise because they disobeyed God, disobedience we inherit. Christian theology built the doctrine of 'original sin' from the idea of a first act of transgression against God having inherited consequences. Nowadays the story in Genesis is seen as a parable of sin affirming our separation from God through unbelief and pride from the start of human consciousness of him. One difficulty for us in reading Saint Paul is the contrast made between Adam and Christ given the contrast in historicity of the two. Paul, like many up to today, accept Adam as an historical figure (Genesis 4:25). Adam though is the Hebrew word for man and can be thought of as named on behalf of humanity as a whole. He and Eve question what God says and follow the invitation to disobey him, lured to 'be like God' (Genesis 3:5). Disbelieving, discontent with being just God's children, out of pride they try to take God's place. This description of Adam's sin is contrasted with the obedience of Jesus whom Paul describes as 'last Adam', the second man ever to be completely without sin. 'The first man, Adam, became a living being; the last Adam became a life-giving spirit'.

Earlier Paul has announced God's historical action in Jesus dealing with the sin and death associated with Adam: 'for as all die in Adam, so all will be made alive in Christ' (1 Corinthians 15:45, 22).

What is the difference between sin and sins? Sin is the tendency away from God and sins are its outcome in individual lives. Just as scripture clarifies these terms, the Holy Spirit shows them up in our lives, so we can repent of sin and welcome deeper conversion to God. Sin refers to a powerful reality within us which, like a tree, brings forth fruit which are our sins. These are an offence against God, whose 'eyes are too pure to behold evil' (Habakkuk 1:13), but also against reason, truth and informed conscience. The good news of Christianity is simple. God made us for friendship. Sin became a barrier to that friendship. God sent Jesus to lift away that barrier, when we repent of sin, making us friends of God. Things get between us and God so that we are not at one. Sin, fear, sickness, bondage, anxiety, death and the devil get in the way. Jesus brings atonement, 'at-one-ment' literally, because what he did in his coming, suffering, death and resurrection established the means to overcome these evils if we use them. 'You are to name him Jesus, for he will save his people from their sins' (Matthew 1:21). The coming of such a Saviour was prophesied by Isaiah: 'he has borne our infirmities and carried our diseases' which comes true when we trust Christ's healing power. When we read 'he bore the sins of many' that can become true in our experience when we seek the forgiveness he won for us on the Cross (Isaiah 53:4,12). If knowledge of sin goes hand in hand with knowledge of God's mercy the record of Christ's sufferings is our greatest teacher. There we see sins of hatred in the crowd, unbelief in the authorities and cowardice in the disciples fleeing from their Lord. Some of these sins were dealt with after Christ's resurrection as the disciples repented of their sinful failings, welcomed the forgiveness of sins and walked forward in the power of the Holy Spirit.

The forward draw of divine love shown in Jesus competes with the backward draw of 'the sin that clings so closely'. There have been different categories of sin made over the centuries. 'Mortal (deadly) sin' is forsaking the forward journey, turning your back to the love of God in a decided action. Since sin is the consequence of freedom gifted by God such a decision is seen as having eternal consequence as it is reversible on the human side only up to death. 'Venial (forgivable) sin' is more typical of the power of sin to pull at our feet as we move forward. There are various lists of sin in scripture condensed in church teaching to seven roots. Human beings are pulled back from God by pride, anger, lust, envy, gluttony, avarice and sloth. Someone made up a mnemonic for these - 'pale gas' - capturing their deadly impact in a comparison with chlorine. These seven deadly or capital sins provide backwards drag of different kinds. For some of us the drag lies in sloth, laziness as we get older. For others there is a weight of indulgence in gluttony. Or there is stubborn refusal to go forward other than on our own terms, pride, seen as the 'sin of youth', that sinks relationships. Then there is the greed taking our eyes away from God's forward invitation and getting them fixated on perishable things. As we struggle with our relationships, insecurities and spiritual emptiness we recognise a more profound struggle against the backwards drag of sin. We struggle in our own strength to shake off our sins when we take our eyes off Jesus, 'the pioneer and perfecter of our faith'. Through his resurrection he always stands before us, breaking the power of sins we confess by his forgiveness and anticipating for us the sight of God ahead. 'When he is revealed, we will be like him, for we will see him as he is. And all who have this hope in him purify themselves, just as he is pure. (1John 3:2-3)

20
So many denominations

'You Christians are so divided how can I know which if any have got it right?' This is one of the biggest and hardest questions Christians have to elucidate. Some whilst lamenting the structural divisions come close to shrugging off the question saying disunity does not ultimately matter. Different denominations, different styles and even different theological beliefs in the church is not in itself division, they say, but a celebration of the rich diversity of church life. True Christians are known to God alone as there is no true church. Other Christians hold that the visible church is part of the gospel so visible church unity is essential. Roman Catholic, Orthodox and Anglocatholic thinking says with St. Paul that 'because there is one bread, we who are many are one body, because we all partake of the one bread' (1 Corinthians 10:17). Christian unity is when people are in communion, or literally can take communion, with the local bishop who is a successor of the apostles.

Whichever view held the divisions of the church are lamented and for many outsiders present a serious obstacle to Christian belief. They seem to say Christianity does not work in practice. This shortfall is seen as especially serious when the Founder of Christianity is recorded as praying in these words for his church 'May they all be one. As you, Father, are in me and I am in you, may they also be in us, so that the world may believe that you have sent me' (John 17:21).

Despite the sad reality of Christian divisions in recent years almost all Christian denominations have entered dialogue with other traditions. The Holy Spirit has been rebuilding the unity of Christians. In 1982 virtually all Christian traditions signed up in Lima to a statement on Baptism, Eucharist and Ministry sponsored by the World Council of Churches. This document identifies the basic elements of the faith of the church through the ages and explains the different approaches across traditions to baptism, the eucharist and ministry. 'We have not yet fully reached "consensus"... understood here as that experience of life and articulation of faith necessary to realise and maintain the Church's visible unity... [though] listening to each other, and jointly returning to the primary sources, namely "the tradition of the Gospel testified in Scripture, transmitted in and by the Church through the power of the Holy Spirit" (Faith and Order World Conference, 1963)' (52). The agreed text has alongside it a commentary explaining differences such as over infant baptism, the change in the elements at the eucharist and the necessity for bishops, priests and deacons. Apart from this document denominations have continued bilateral discussion so that very strong convergence was reached in documentation between Anglicans and Roman Catholics. Ironically, after the ordination of women in the former, hospitality by RCs to those who moved in consequence to the latter broke new ground in ecumenism. Pope Benedict XVI's 2009 Apostolic Constitution providing for Anglican Ordinariates comes close to a healing of the English Reformation in accepting the validity of many aspects of Anglican tradition. The Anglocatholic vision behind the Ordinariate traces back to the 19th century Oxford Movement through the 1920s Malines Conversations to be disoriented by changes both in the RC and Anglican churches since 1960.

Though now on the margins the catholic vision of Anglicanism provides clear ethical teaching, encourages sacramental life and challenges innovations to confession, marriage and ordination in the name of the wider church, Roman Catholic and Orthodox. Since synodical government was introduced in 1970 an enormous burden has been placed on parish priests in having to teach the Faith in a qualified manner pointing to the official acceptance of variety in fairly important matters such as marriage and ordination. There remains a distinction between those who see ordination as of the 'esse' (essential to) and those who see it as of the 'bene esse' (beneficial to) the Church alongside those who are undecided on this. The genius of Anglicanism for being 'catholic and reformed' now has a downside in an uneasy alliance of Anglocatholic and Evangelical with Middle of the Road bishops keeping the peace on divisive issues. As Anglocatholics do their best to stick to their mother Church they are seeing it as an ecumenical body in which, to quote Vatican II, full Christian Faith 'subsists' in the midst of much dilution and distortion of It. Some others see Anglicans as part of a conservative Church seeking to conserve a position in an agnostic society that has strayed a long way from Christian allegiance! In elucidating Anglicanism its reliance on the 'three legged stool' of scripture, tradition and reason shows up a similar obedience to the faith of the church through the ages to that voiced in the Lima document. The problem is less theory than practice in finding the best accommodation of the sections of Christianity to one another within a fast moving culture.

Since 1985 Greek housewife Mrs. Vassula Ryden claims to have received 'locutions' or messages from Jesus. Over the last 35 years tens of thousands have come to recognise in her messages a respelling of the call of the scriptures to repentance and faith in Jesus and a fresh owning of Our Lord's call for the sundered branches of his church to come together. Readers of the messages form a network active in prayer, evangelisation and works of charity called True Life in God (TLIG) in many nations. They speak of God's desire for spiritual renewal - building invisible unity among believers - and recovering the visible unity of his church. The inner power of the Church is presented as the Holy Spirit alongside a picture of the three main branches of the church – catholic, orthodox and protestant – as three metal bars needing bending and uniting together by the white heat of the Spirit. Until this happens, the divine messages say, God's work of reconciling the world is held back. The messages are a call to unceasing prayer, for churches to unite in diversity and work together in evangelisation for the conversion of the world. Many in TLIG and beyond see the ecumenical ministry of the Pope, working closely with the Orthodox Ecumenical Patriarch and the Archbishop of Canterbury, as a gift of God in this respect (53).

'Christ loved the church and gave himself up for her in order to ...present her to himself in splendour, without spot or wrinkle...that she may be holy and without blemish' (Ephesians 5:25-27). Through all the events of human history there is a divine agenda revealed in scripture and confirmed by prophecy centred upon uniting and perfecting the church. Jesus the heavenly bridegroom is preparing his church as a bride. The whole history of the world is a servant of this task. Why then are Christians so divided? Because even if the church is a divine institution she is also human and sinful. There has been a battle between the humanity and divinity of the church right across the centuries. 2000 years on there is holiness in the church even if it is still filled with sinful people!

The church is God's never ending family called by him to proclaim the whole faith to the whole world. This calling is being achieved despite her failings. Christian unity is most evident in local congregations which have been called 'the hope of the world' (Bill Hybels). If you join a church you become part of a living hope. If you join a church, because you are a sinner, you also do damage to Christian unity. There is no perfect church because there are no perfect Christians. Nowadays there are few denominations that would say they have got it exactly right. Despite past behaviour very few sections of the church totally exclude any other.

Every branch of the church is by definition partial and so falls short. This has been a practical discovery for many. When years back Archbishop Desmond Tutu was asked how the Christian denominations in South Africa succeeded in uniting to lead the fight against apartheid he commented that apartheid was too powerful a foe for disunited churches. God gave a practical unity across denominations that focussed and strengthened the Christian challenge to racial discrimination. The fight against social injustice brings the churches together in the cause of Christ's kingdom.

Despite argument, disrespect, breaking of communion and an unwillingness to work together by Christians there is also much love in the church. Jesus said 'by your love for one another you will be known as my disciples'. He also pledged to keep providing that love by the continual outpouring of his Holy Spirit. Through that gift Christians remain open to welcome the gifts of God in other traditions especially those, like the office of the Pope, traditional head of the Church claiming the authority granted Peter by Christ (Matthew 16:18-19), which have the capacity to further the visible union of Christians one with another.

21
So many faiths

I come across people who believe in God but will not sign up to a religion either due to the hypocrisy they read of or to confusion about which of many religions is most credible. People today are more aware of the variety of faiths across the world than their parents or grandparents through the revolution in global communications over the last half century. With so many faiths to choose from, they rightly ask, how do you decide which one is right? Elucidating, shedding light on the variety of faiths, risks being patronising towards faiths I have not known from the inside. I am impelled to do so by a conviction that the instinct for meaning, and hence religion, is in every human heart. This surely is why our species is called 'homo sapiens', translated 'man who is wise'. I sense God's love and holiness at work in believers from other faiths than my own, let alone unbelievers, and see how they contribute to the common good of society. They do so by upholding values such as compassion and truthfulness that derive from their vision of God and humanity. With the decline in religious practice in the UK people's lives are being formed alarmingly more by what is legal, whether that be right or wrong, and the widespread influence of marketing, rather than by the moral framework owned by religion. This makes elucidation about how we see different faiths all the more important.

Should we have so many faiths - or any faiths? American professor of Jurisprudence Brian Leiter makes a salvo against tolerating religion at all questioning what he sees as the irrational and morally questionable nature of the variety of revelations of the divine. Why should a Sikh boy be permitted to take his ceremonial knife to school and not a farmer's boy? Leiter challenges the legal protection afforded religious belief in western democracies asking why concerns of safety are made subordinate to its claims. His thesis builds on widely publicised bad behaviour of religious adherents to present a view that the common good, which law serves, needs purifying of the metaphysical element altogether as being not just beyond but destructively against reason. In his analysis Brian Leiter details religious beliefs as distinct from other beliefs in being not based on evidence and issuing in categorical demands even if they provide 'existential consolation'. The conclusion of Leiter's argument is that the state should tolerate religious claims of conscience but not give them the respect given them hitherto which subordinates the morally important objectives of safety, health, well-being and equal treatment before the law to such claims. The Sikh boy should surrender his dagger. Since religion serves cohesion in communities of faith it can also contribute to social division when people of different faith attempt to co-exist. The consequent conflicts fuel a perception, articulated by Leiter, that holding to faith is damaging and therefore mistaken. His arguments are parallel to those against the internet for fuelling partisan behaviour which discount its positive achievements in promoting the common good by putting so people in touch with one another (54).

At the other end of reflection on many faiths from this 'plague on all your houses' view are those who hold only their religion to be true and all others totally false. One thinks of 'door to door religion sales folk' like Jehovah's Witnesses who will brook no dialogue. Years back Roman Catholics were said to hold 'outside the church there is no salvation' but now clearly deny this with recent teaching accepting in some degree the baptised of any Church and looking positively, from a salvation angle, on all who follow their conscience. A third perspective seems currently more fashionable than either dismissal of religion overall or dismissal of non-adherents of one's own faith. It affirms all faiths are true so that contradictions between them are superficial. This Hindu parable captures its sense. 'There were five blind Hindu holy men on the banks of the Ganges. A tame elephant wandered among them one day. One reached out and touched its body; he thought it was a wall of mud. One touched its tusks and thought these were two spears. One touched its trunk and thought it was a serpent. One touched its tail and thought it was a piece of rope. The last one laughed at them and held onto its leg. He said it was a tree after all. A child walked by and asked, 'Why are you all holding the elephant?' The story denies obvious contradictions between the truth claims of different faiths (55).

Holding that all religions are true in what they agree about is an attractive thesis, as are attempts at identifying a hierarchy of truth across faiths even if this goes counter to irreconcilable claims of divine revelation. Though people of faith have different views of God, there is agreement among devoted adherents about how partial a view they all have got. God is bigger than our vision of God and that of all religions. People of faith are agreed on the failings of hypocrisy, adherents whose nit-picking legalism seems unworthy of the Creator, of whom it would be just to say 'their God is too small'. By contrast there is much holiness among religious people. This connects with the idea 'all religions lead to God' proving religions help people encounter God and, so to speak, brush off holiness from him. In that sense, of creating holiness, no religion is completely right or wrong. However holy people can be mistaken. It is possible to follow fruitfully the truth you have received, to the best of your ability, only to one day wake up to find you're following a shadow of the truth. I remember reading the story of a Muslim lady who thought you reached God by moral effort until she discovered in Jesus Christ with great joy how we grow into a personal relationship with God not by effort but by his grace. This emphasis on grace leads some strains of Christianity to disavow the name of religion and its association with ritual practice almost as an insurance policy concerning one's eternal destiny. Mainstream Churches though recognise common ground with other faiths concerning the vision of God despite awareness of undeniable disagreements. In Christianity God is seen as having a closeness or sameness to us alongside a distance or difference from us, expressed respectively as immanence and transcendence. In holding together God's closeness yet otherness, his sameness yet difference, Christianity is in the middle of the spectrum of world religions. These range from the strongly transcendent vision of God in Islam and Judaism to the more immanent devotion found in Hindu and Buddhist societies which currently has great impact in the UK through meditation and mindfulness exercises borrowed from those sources.

In John chapter 14, verse 6 Christ said: 'I am the way, the truth and the life; no one comes to the Father except through me' and in Chapter 18 v38; 'Everyone who is of the truth hears my voice.' If everyone believed those scriptures there would be no need to elucidate how Christians see other faiths because they would not exist!. Putting it in a more challenging way to Christians the existence of other religions is proof of their failure to meet with Jesus at a deep level and become the heart to heart draw they are meant to be through his magnetic love. What though of those who're drawn elsewhere? My book 'Meet Jesus' has this section on how a Christian might see people who follow other faiths: 'Saying yes to Jesus does not mean saying 'no' to everything about other faiths. It can mean saying 'yes, but...' or rather 'yes, and...' to other faiths, which is a far more engaging and reasonable attitude. I say 'yes' to what Buddhists teach about detachment because Jesus teaches it and Christians often forget it. At the same time I must respectfully question Buddhists about the lack of a personal vision of God since I believe Jesus is God's Son. I say 'yes' to what Muslims say about God's majesty because sometimes Christians seem to domesticate God and forget his awesome nature. At the same time, I differ with Muslims about how we gain salvation, because I believe Jesus is God's salvation gift and more than a prophet. Other faiths can wake us up to aspects of Christian truth that might otherwise get forgotten. What might happen, for example, if Christians were as serious in their spiritual discipline as many Buddhists are?' (56) Reflection upon experience of people of faith in our circle and the good seen in them like humility and self-forgetfulness can be profitable as a reminder of how people can live close to God outside the Church. To the question 'Can religion lead you to God?' biblical faith says yes in the sense of religion expressing love in return for love. In Christianity God leads us to God. 'For God so loved the world that he gave his only Son, so that everyone who believes in him may not perish but may have eternal life' (John 3:16).

22
Suffering

The coronavirus pandemic has been a repressing force like a brake or imprisoning ball and chain. Barred from leaving home without necessity we felt like caged hamsters on the wheel of a routine going round and round looking forward to release from both cage and wheel. The pain of our isolation was amplified by the suffering and deaths of family and friends we kept distance from following unassailable yet heartbreaking logic. In a pandemic we cannot do what we want to do for our sake and for the sake of others. Societies that accept, or have to accept, heavy regulation from government have accommodated better to this than open societies where restricting freedom to do as you like seems alien. Stepping away from people on the pavement is now ingrained and lack of intimacy with others is having widespread effect on mental health. It is a painful scenario at the time of writing although vaccinations bring hope of reducing the pain of coronavirus to something like the annual onslaught of influenza. Living through a pandemic puts pay to entertainments we take for granted like going to the theatre or a football match. For others the pandemic has impacted far beyond that, taking the lives of hospital staff, bus drivers and many who work on the front line of public services. The Christian response to coronavirus has been to offer prayer for its removal, care for its victims and wisdom on the creative bearing of suffering.

It is something of a paradox to pray against something whilst accepting the suffering it brings. The coronavirus pandemic as a natural disaster raises questions about divine love and power. Accepting God's love, Christians pray to him to exercise his power to eradicate the virus. At the same time we encourage believers who suffer to trust the love of God and believe 'that all things work together for good for those who love God, who are called according to his purpose' (Romans 8:28). The link between the two responses is conviction that God has a long term plan into which we have to weave our aspirations including making the most of suffering. I recall little Brandon from my last parish, only five, who died of a brain tumour. I both baptised and buried him and still share the grief of his family. To believe in a good God in the face of Brandon's passing seemed alien to some. To others, including his mother, who put faith in God's working, such belief was a lifeline. Her testimony presented tangible evidence of how faith brings blessing through suffering, as Jesus showed on the Cross. Dorothy Sayers, besides being famous as a crime writer, was a child of the Vicarage and fervent Christian. She was well aware, writing shortly after the Second World War, of the challenge to God people saw in suffering. In this passage from her book 'Creed or Chaos?' she speaks powerfully of the significance of Jesus: 'For whatever reason God chose to make man as he is - limited and suffering and subject to sorrow and death - he had the honesty and the courage to take his own medicine. Whatever game he is playing with his creation, he has kept his own rules and played fair. He can exact nothing from man that he has not exacted from himself. He has himself gone through the whole of human experience, from the trivial irritations of family life and the cramping restrictions of hard work and lack of money to the worst horrors of pain and humiliation, defeat, despair and death. When he was a man, he played the man. He was born in poverty and died in disgrace and thought it well worthwhile' (57).

There is no knock-down argument that can make sense of things like the death of a five year old or coronavirus but through faith in Jesus we find ground to stand on as we do our best to live in a world where suffering is so real. If I rejected the existence of a loving God in favour of cruel fate I would have other problems explaining the existence of all the love that flows in the world, as into Brandon's household, and into care of so many with lives impacted by coronavirus. Timothy Keller makes a succinct observation: 'If you have a God great and transcendent enough to be mad at because he hasn't stopped evil and suffering in the world... you have... a God great and transcendent enough to have good reasons for allowing it to continue that you can't know... you can't have it both ways' (58). Like love, suffering takes us beyond reason.

To say 'suffering disproves God' sounds reasonable, but life, and God who made life, take us beyond reason. It is natural to wish for an end to suffering and for evil to be banished but since human beings are blemished there would be no hope for us if God banned evil. If you condemn the Creator for the wickedness in the world you are condemning him for granting human beings the freedom to mess up. As an example, though a great number of website 'hits' are on pornographic sites could we make that an excuse to condemn the internet altogether when it hosts so much of value? If we condemn people overall on account of the way some misuse their freedom we ignore the good deeds of others balancing their bad deeds. God made both Maximilian Kolbe and Adolf Hitler. It was Hitler who sanctioned the wickedness of Auschwitz. The Polish priest Fr Kolbe was sent there because he sheltered Jews. When a prisoner escaped, the camp commandant ordered ten men to be chosen for execution. Kolbe offered himself in exchange for a married man and died instead of him. The love that flowed from Maximilian Kolbe brightened the darkness of Hitler's death camp. The good use of freedom in one cannot be weighed directly against the evil consequences of the other's misdoing yet the light it sheds on suffering is undeniable.

'Are any among you suffering? They should pray. Are any cheerful? They should sing songs of praise. Are any among you sick? They should call for the elders of the church and have them pray over them, anointing them with oil in the name of the Lord. The prayer of faith will save the sick, and the Lord will raise them up; and anyone who has committed sins will be forgiven. Therefore confess your sins to one another, and pray for one another, so that you may be healed' (James 5:13-16). In this scripture passage suffering is addressed directly. It gives a call to pray in penitence expecting relief, of sickness in particular, and to lay hands and anoint the sufferer. The sacrament of anointing finds its authority here, an outward ceremony seen as the major Christian instrument of healing. As a priest I often see an immediate effect from this rite, especially as people approach it with expectancy upon God to act. Ministering in the interior of Guyana, often a long way from medical care, I sometimes saw malaria lift in an instant through such prayer. On other occasions it has been the occasion for a dying person to make their surrender and pass speedily to God. Healing is a cure but more than that, just as suffering is more than physical pain. Christian ministry to those who are hurting builds from the instinctive laying on of hands everyone does themselves or to one to another after an injury. The voice of prayer and pouring of oil calls upon the healing embrace of God so well represented in the earthly life of Jesus. That God, when asked in the name of Jesus, acts to heal is central to the Christian good news, be that action a cure, a building of faith to bear suffering or granting grace to submit to death. The Christian response to suffering has many facets, spiritual, medical, practical and political, linked to hurt in body, mind, spirit and relationships in humans, animals as well as the environment. The global coronavirus pandemic has seen people of all nations and creeds brought together in the task of alleviating suffering across the world. That work for Christians flows from conviction that God in Christ reduces despair to sadness through the Cross, a sadness caused by empathy with so many in pain yoked to the hope of redemption. 'The Spirit bears witness with our spirit that we are children of God, and if children, then heirs, heirs of God and joint heirs with Christ - if, in fact, we suffer with him so that we may also be glorified with him. I consider that the sufferings of this present time are not worth comparing with the glory about to be revealed to us. For the creation waits with eager longing for the revealing of the children of God' (Romans 8:16-19).

23
The Empty Tomb

There is no proof of Christ's resurrection, only strong evidence. That is the case for any past event. Belief in the resurrection of Jesus stems from the faith of the church and an accumulation of evidence. In past ages its significance was limited to proving the divinity of Christ so that his birth was the incarnation of God and his suffering the overcoming of sin and death. Nowadays Christ's resurrection is seen as more central than confirmatory both to the church's transformational dynamic and to apologetics, the reasoned defence or 'apologia' of Christian faith. Christianity stands or falls on the event which has a documented history whilst being a metaphysical ('beyond the natural') event with significance beyond history. Defending the resurrection we sail 'between the Scylla of critical pedantry and the Charybdis of vaguely religious psychology' (Rowan Williams). If we make the establishing of the empty tomb narratives our goal that can reduce to pedantry because it is not the prime issue which is 'who left that tomb and where can he be found?' If we make the resurrection just a symbol of love's triumph, bringing meaning to suffering and so on we also make it less than it is as a metaphysical event rooted in history. Shedding light on, elucidating Christ's resurrection has an eye to the faith of the church through the ages alongside historical scholarship and the life of the church as the community of the resurrection with a meaning and power beyond itself (59).

In a few sentences we can make broad brush strokes about the truth of the resurrection. I would put first the existence of a community founded on the resurrection with a dynamic inexplicable without it. Josephus, Pliny and Tacitus give independent evidence for the remarkable growth of the church after Christ's death. Then, secondly, the credibility of the New Testament witness to the resurrection which has survived two centuries of critical scholarship. The New Testament record of how Christ's sad and defeated disciples were changed into fearless missionaries is hard to explain without a cataclysmic external impact upon their lives. Minor inconsistencies in the accounts of the resurrection seem to reflect less their being a fabrication and more their being halting attempts to describe a hereto unimaginable event. The role of women as witnesses is controversial for those days and would not have been included in any fabricated story. The abandonment by devout Jews of a weekly tradition of Friday Sabbath to keep Sunday as the day of resurrection has no rival explanation. Lastly there is no grave venerated for the founder of Christianity compared to founders of other religions, only the empty tomb in Jerusalem. These considerations are brush strokes painting a picture of an event pointing beyond itself to the unique action of God in raising Jesus from the dead, the pledge of an imperishable hope held to by a third of the world's population today.

No one saw the resurrection. We have no eye witnesses or videos. It is not strictly a historical event but metaphysical. Though his friends and enemies saw his crucifixion before their eyes, after that encounter with Jesus entered another realm. This Spirit-filled existence went beyond mere resuscitation of his corpse to make him the source of eternal life to humankind. What happened on Easter Day comes down to us due to a series of transformative encounters with the risen Lord tracing back to the discovery of his empty tomb. Those encounters ceased after a time to continue in a different mode by the descent of the Holy Spirit which is inseparable from Easter. The meaning and power of scripture and sacrament today are linked to Easter, words and signs continuing to manifest the risen presence of Jesus when believers gather in his name. Though the resurrection of Jesus goes beyond history, the witness to it by the apostles and other disciples is historical. It is a solid witness based on the Gospels, the Acts of the Apostles and the writings of St Paul who makes this summary: 'I handed on to you as of first importance what I in turn had received: that Christ died for our sins in accordance with the scriptures, and that he was buried, and that he was raised on the third day in accordance with the scriptures, and that he appeared to Cephas, then to the twelve. Then he appeared to more than five hundred brothers and sisters at one time, most of whom are still alive, though some have died. Then he appeared to James, then to all the apostles. Last of all, as to one untimely born, he appeared also to me' (1 Corinthians 15:3-8).

In weighing up the historicity of the empty tomb one problem is that the references to the tomb are in the Gospel accounts written at least 20 years after the first letters of Paul which give little reference to the tomb save the reference above to Christ's burial. Paul's witness to the resurrection builds from his own encounter with the risen Lord Jesus which he associates with those of the apostles at Easter. So central is the resurrection to Paul's thought that Acts 17:18 relates 'he was telling the good news about Jesus and the resurrection'. Some opponents of Christianity see this preaching as built on Paul's subjective visionary experiences and not on the history of Jesus, his death and resurrection. Against that perception we can point to Paul's writings as the earliest witness to the resurrection (Romans 4:24f, 6:4, 6:9, 7:4, 8:11, 29, 34, 10:9; 1 Corinthians 6:14, 15:4, 12-17, 20, 29, 32, 35, 42-44, 52; 2 Corinthians 1:9, 4:14, 5:15; Galatians 1:1; Ephesians 1:20; Colossians 2:12; 1 Thessalonians 1:10). Such a witness to Jesus who died and rose that we might die to sin and rise to new life in the Spirit seems inseparable from the memory of Christ. The resurrection is something in Christian experience because it was the experience of Jesus.

That the writings of Paul do not directly mention the empty tomb does not mean the writer was not aware of and formed by the same events as the Gospel writers. The physical elements of Christ's resurrection are underlined in later New Testament writings which describe the discovery of the empty tomb alongside encounters involving Jesus speaking (John 21:15-22), touching (John 20:27) and eating (Luke 24:41-43). Whereas Paul's resurrection experience was visionary and non-physical the accounts in the Gospels are very different, stressing, especially in Luke and John, the physical aspects. That both the Gospels and Paul's letters are in the New Testament is a reminder of their complementary witness to the spiritual and physical aspects of faith in Christ's resurrection. As Paul's experience of the risen Lord on the Damascus Road exemplifies, the strong tradition of the empty tomb is secondary to that of the appearances of Jesus to individuals when it comes to resurrection faith. It was seeing Jesus that helped the apostles and others make sense of his empty tomb. Resurrection faith then and now is spiritual and physical for both Jesus and those who trust in him, a resurrection inside of us after repentance and baptism and anticipated for our bodies at Christ's return. 'Therefore we have been buried with him by baptism into death, so that, just as Christ was raised from the dead by the glory of the Father, so we too might walk in newness of life. For if we have been united with him in a death like his, we will certainly be united with him in a resurrection like his' (Romans 6:4-5).

In Lent 2018 I made it my challenge to prepare 40 pointers to Christ's resurrection to release daily in Easter Season on social media blog accompanied by classic paintings of the risen Lord with captions setting forth evidence for the truth of Easter. This blog can be accessed at https://40resurrectionpointers.blogspot.com. It summarises to an extent a month long debate I had some years back with an atheist prominent on social media who wanted someone to engage with about the truth of the resurrection. In that debate I became more aware that, though Christ proved his resurrection to the first disciples, we can only highlight pointers to its truth as I have attempted here and in my earlier book 'Pointers to Heaven' (60). There is no knock down proof of a past event but that of Christ's resurrection needs pondering and with openness to wider metaphysical questions that reach out from it. Is the evidence for Christ's resurrection trustworthy or is it not? Is Jesus the Son of God or is he not? Are you and I destined for eternal splendour or not? As Alexander Schmemann affirms: 'The only meaningful thing in life is what conquers death, and not "what" but "who" - Christ. There is undoubtedly only one joy: to know him and share him with each other' (61).

24
Trusting the Church

The Church is God given yet man-handled. As God's never-ending family it has unique status tracing back twenty centuries across five continents. It is an instrument of salvation conveying Christ's divinity. It is also human in a deficient sense compared to her sinless Lord. With 24-7 media scrutiny people are more aware than ever of those failings, especially clerical abuse of people for sexual gratification. Trusting the Church, an essential for Christians, has been made a mockery in our age and an uphill struggle to elucidate. Despite clerical failings however scripture makes these invitations: 'we appeal to you, brothers and sisters, to respect those who labour among you, and have charge of you in the Lord and admonish you; esteem them very highly in love because of their work' (1 Thessalonians 5:12-13) 'Obey your leaders and submit to them, for they are keeping watch over your souls and will give an account. Let them do this with joy and not with sighing - for that would be harmful to you' (Hebrews 13:17). In such words we are encouraged to distrust ourselves and look to those trained and authorised to engage us with the word of God, in the worship of the eucharist and moral wisdom of the church through the ages. The alternative is going our own way without sermons, eucharists, moral guidance or formation in prayer all of which build divine life within us to the detriment of our sinful humanity. More than that, essential to being a Christian is being part of the community, the local body of Christ, in corporate engagement with scripture, eucharist, the age old expression of faith and morals, under pastoral oversight.

What does it mean to trust the Church? Who or what do we trust? Any community with a purpose is held on track by appropriate authority. The Christian Church claims to have been given authority by Jesus Christ to continue his saving mission of bringing all that is into fellowship with God. We trust the Scriptures, Creeds, liturgical texts, Bishops in ordered succession in many traditions and Church Councils to hold us today to that saving mission. Trusting the Church involves recognising and submitting to the exercise of these tested instruments of the living Christ interpreted to us in the local Christian community. In a fast-changing world the discerning of what has ultimate authority is a perilous activity. It is a process confused by naive exercise of authority and the capacity of mass media to distort and ridicule legitimate authority. The divisions of the Church are evident and weaken her authority overall even if there is greater understanding and appreciation of her different streams. To outsiders they are no encouragement to trust the Church but invite a decision to trust - make a plunge into - one of the streams hopeful of catching their flow and being supported by it. Such plunges are, looking across the different flows, submission primarily to scripture (Evangelical), experience of the Holy Spirit (Pentecostal), age old liturgy and bishops (Orthodox), The Pope and bishops (Roman Catholic).

Anglicans in principle trust the authority of bishops but choice of parish can be more influential. The Church of England is defined as 'catholic and reformed' with high Anglicans owning more the former (cf RC/Orthodox), low Anglicans the latter (cf Evangelical/Protestant) and middle-of-the-road Anglicans a mixture often with more of an eye than the other two to what is more appealing to the local community. Trusting the Church as Anglicans implies holding to the faith and practice of the Church through the ages and its fresh expression consonant with scripture and what people are thinking in the world around us. This can make decision making difficult since Anglicans like most Protestants have introduced in recent years a strong element of democracy in church governance. The exercise of authority in the Christian tradition is not basically democratic as it is handed from God. Whilst Anglicans would never vote out the Ten Commandments we look to both reasoned consideration and revealed faith to guide establishing a consensus on issues. Episcopally led but synodically governed Anglicans struggle again and again for that consensus. The bishops are from their office custodians of revealed faith in synods which often argue that the Holy Spirit is speaking through the world around the Church to bring change. Failure to attain consensus on the marriage of divorced people within the lifetime of their spouses, the ordination of women and the dedication of same-sex unions las led to qualified approval of each since some Anglicans see them as unauthorised innovation and others as authoritative development. Making decisions on such matters as one small part of the universal Church means the decisions get qualified to honour the wider constituency and Anglicans who look to it.

Many would rather think for themselves than grant loyalty to any stream of the Christian Church despite the danger of trusting one's own intuition geared as it often is to questionable self interest. As a teenager I was aware of Christian teaching, for example on sexual ethics, and had the example and commendation of this of both my parents. There was also a level of detachment. With that came fascination with Anglocatholic worship through which as a student I found a more robust Anglicanism seeing the Church as a dynamic movement which drew me in at more cost to myself. Seeing holy people close at hand influenced me. I aspired to the faith they practised, the cohesion of worship, doctrine, ethics and devotion and seeing oneself immersed in the wider flow of the universal Church. This was my first trusting the Church and it came with heart and soul. Looking back I am grateful for my 'mothering' by the Church and the way it has helped me live as a better child of God our Father. Discernment at different stages of my life, especially about ordination and marriage, has linked to respecting counsel given by those with authority over me as bishops, priests or spiritual directors. After ordination I served in two parishes and then started to pray about marriage. To my surprise this coincided with an invitation from the Bishop of Guyana in South America to me as a single priest to help train indigenous clergy. I accepted serving this obvious need with rather a heavy heart. To cut the story short I met my wife, Anne in the process who greatly helped the training. On our return from Guyana, experience training priests equipped me to be a diocesan officer working for church growth alongside clergy in London and then Sussex. I recall helping churches develop evangelistic engagement and how surveys of new church members evidenced them being drawn across spiritual and practical hurdles into two convictions: God is good and the Church is OK. Business with God leads people so far but it needs complementing by a decision to trust the Church and give the institution the benefit of the doubt. As in my own experience, seeing the integrity, large-heartedness and holiness of church members can be pivotal in overcoming the stereotypes of Christians as narrow thinking.

Why trust the Church? It can look as if entry into the Church is by such a narrow entrance that space inside looks unlikely to be greater. 'Enter through the narrow gate... for the gate is narrow and the road is hard that leads to life, and there are few who find it' (Matthew 7:13, 14). Those words of Jesus imply once loyalty is granted to him it leads to life and space even if it squeezes out a lot. When we hear a concert pianist practice hour by hour they also appear on a narrow path but attending the concert shows us the fruitful significance of that narrowing. Trusting the Church as she takes the time, talents and money of her members is a similar act of faith. Not that Christianity requires blind loyalty. As in all families loyalty within God's family is allowed to be critical but, hopefully, with an eye to building consensus. With a momentum stretching back through twenty centuries Christianity has a natural conservatism. This wards off challenge to its authority, as a wise parent stands her ground against teenage children. All of this is saying that despite its suspicion both of 'worldly' thinking and radical thinking within her, the Christian Church has space for dissent. There is an infuriating saying that the Church thinks in centuries. All the same Christianity, with its doctrine that God took on human flesh, is so rooted in the world that its consensus of belief and practice shifts over time. Such developments often occur through the acceptance of views which had originally been expressed in a spirit of 'loyal dissent'. One of the basic characteristics of Christian philosophy is a refusal to pass hasty judgements on other people, and this may help to explain how the Church has managed to maintain its cohesion despite the many differences over doctrine. Those who live within mainstream Christianity often see it as much more humble and questioning, at times even agnostic than it appears to be from the outside.

JOHN TWISLETON

25
Unanswered prayer

In her best selling novel 'Just My Luck' Adele Parks weaves a tale about winning the lottery. It has the sub-title 'What if winning means losing everything' and chronicles the impact on Lexi and Jake and their circle of winning £18 million. For fifteen years they have played the same six numbers with two other couples. Just prior to drawing the winning ticket there had been a rift in the group so their friends are seemingly ineligible to gain part of the bounty. It is a gripping tale playing on what many see as the biggest answer to prayer and how unsatisfactory that answer can be (62). Prayer to God is set forth by Christ as analogous to children's requests to their parents. I am aware as a parent how difficult it can be answering requests for money from your children. Sometimes they ask you with fingers crossed, like the symbol of the National Lottery, hoping luck will prevail. Though crossed fingers go back to pre-Christian times they are resonant of an essential of Christian prayer, that it be in the name of Jesus i.e. a generous prayer. Is praying to win the Lottery such a prayer? Many who buy their tickets with crossed fingers and aspiration to heaven think of what they would give to others if they won. They are ready to live with unanswered prayer week by week content at the small proportion of their purchase that goes to charity. Others see any form of giving in hope of a return as against the grain of Christianity and look more directly to God to resource them including their service of the needy in their circle.

Is unanswered prayer unsurprising or challenging? Just as millions pray unsuccessfully every week to win the Lottery others pray the Our Father day by day but look rather in vain for the establishing of God's kingdom of justice and peace. Something like a Lottery win is surprising when it happens but so can be the establishing of justice and peace in the world. The difference in the prayers is the challenge to personal investment in the two. One is primarily about being a one-off consumer - buying a ticket in hope of gain - the other is about building a generous attitude as a citizen of God's kingdom. Living with unanswered prayer as a Christian is a struggle linked less to lack of fortune in personal life and more to disappointment about progress in 'the kingdom of the world becom[ing] the kingdom of our Lord and of his Messiah' (Revelation 11:15). Christian prayer flows in gratitude for being part of creation, sorrow for our shortcomings which ruin the world, praise to Jesus sent to remedy these as our redeemer and petition for God to fill our needs. It is a relationship established in 'the love that moves the sun and the other stars' (Dante) and seeks to gather us with all things to itself for kindling. 'I came to bring fire to the earth, and how I wish it were already kindled' (Luke 12:49). Frustration at unanswered prayer is at this highest level disappointment that human beings are as yet not fully aflame with love for God and one another with sad consequences evidenced in lack of justice and peace and disrespect for our environment.

The Christian eucharist has an impatience about it, a yearning for God's kingdom which is building up but sometimes little evident. In the action bread and wine are taken alongside worshippers to be offered as a living prayer in anticipation of fulfilment at Christ's return. 'As often as you eat this bread and drink the cup, you proclaim the Lord's death until he comes' (1 Corinthians 11:26). In recent years involvement in the eucharist has been recapturing this future aspiration, a proclamation of God's love reaching into the future, looking to fulfilment of so many unanswered prayers for humanity to be put into its right mind in preparation for Christ's return. 'Christ in an all-inclusive, cosmic sense gathers all things within him. The open arms of Christ on the cross and his open heart pierced by the wounds of the world can be seen as an immense, cosmic outflowing and gathering in, open to all realities, to all peoples, to all faiths in the embrace of love and the act of feeding. For Christians, this is the centre'. In those words Ursula King summarises the thinking of Teilhard de Chardin whose writings make explicit the unfulfilled yearning of the prayer of the eucharist. In his 'Mass on the World' the invocation of the Holy Spirit at the eucharist is seen as an echo of Christ's desire to 'cast fire upon the earth' and the stellar fires and molten lava that energise the earth's development. In the elevation of the Host at mass Teilhard sees in anticipation the raising up of Jesus as the 'Omega Point' on his return to gather all things to himself (63).

The term 'unanswered prayer' betrays a transactional view of prayer even if the aspect of God supplying our needs is clearly portrayed in scripture. As mentioned the petitionary aspect of prayer stands alongside praise, confession and thanksgiving which by renaming can form the mnemonic ACTS. This prioritises in descending order: adoration, confession, thanksgiving and supplication. The descent links to decreasing God centeredness of aspects. Adoration centres purely on God himself, confession of sin on our unworthiness to face God in his holiness, thanksgiving on what God has given us and supplication centres on our own needs. All these aspects are found in the corporate prayer of worship as at the eucharist. They flow together so that ingratitude and lack of penitence subtract from praise which in turn has impact upon appropriate supplication. Over my life I have found unanswered prayer more surprising as I have learned more about what to ask for. When something I take to God regularly remains unfulfilled after a long time I am now surprised. God as God of all has insight into where a human petition, thought and spoken with readiness to act if needs be, can impact things. Through regular centring upon God at the eucharist and in personal prayer I get schooled in the people and things to bring him at a particular season. The fact that names come onto and then off my prayer list show my prayers are answered. Even then there is no exact science in my relationship with God just as there is no scientific explanation of my marriage and friendships.

Sometimes our relationship with God, like our human relationships, blows cold even if the one to one commitment remains and good things keep flowing one to another. This is described as a 'dark night of the soul' in the sense of losing the sense of God's presence in your life. Spiritual guides can help us interpret this loss as a gift from God's left hand sent to help us love and work for him without spiritual consolation because it is right to do so without immediate gratification. In my book 'Pointers to Heaven' I describe an incident linked to a contemporary saint who wrote about how little they felt God's love in their spirit. 'I read 'Come Be My Light' by Mother Teresa in which the saint writes of the obscuring of her faith. It equipped me to witness heaven to an agnostic gentleman, like me a writer, languishing in hospital with a brain tumour. I was visiting his ward when he engaged me in a conversation which touched on his envy of someone like myself who seemingly could not entertain doubt about heaven. Having listened carefully I said I was not without questions and I'd just read about Mother Teresa's questioning. As I talked a doctor striding through the ward stopped abruptly and turned to us. 'Did I hear you mention Mother Teresa? I trained with her. She gave me this medallion.' He bent down, unbuttoned his shirt and pulled out a holy medal. I was astonished and instinctively touched it, as did my agnostic friend. It was as if the saint was good enough to reach down from heaven to kindle faith in an unbeliever through an extraordinary coincidence' (64). This story has an irony in its evidencing both divine intervention and the importance of keeping a degree of detachment from such spiritual consolations.

In my experience direct answers to prayer, as for help encouraging an agnostic friend, are rare but more common than any benefits I would gain from a Lottery subscription. Unanswered prayer remains a mystery but the millions of prayers and eucharists offered daily hold the world up into the transformative embrace of a God whose invisible reality beyond imagining is made known in Jesus Christ who promised 'if in my name you ask me for anything, I will do it' (John 14:14).

Notes

1 Hans Urs von Balthasar, *Elucidations* (SPCK, 1975 translation by John Riches of 1971 German edition) pp viii, 216
2 Website of Jonathan Sacks 2019 https://rabbisacks.org/choose-not-to-be-a-bystander-but-to-confront-racism-head-on-thought-for-the-day/
3 The Faith and Order Commission of the Church of England, *God's Unfailing Word: Theological and Practical Perspectives on Christian–Jewish Relations* (Church House Publishing, 2019), p3
4 *God's Unfailing Word* p66
5 *God's Unfailing Word* p103
6 Commission for religious relations with the Jews, 'The gifts and the calling of God are irrevocable' (Rom 11:29): A reflection on theological questions pertaining to Catholic-Jewish relations on the occasion of the 50th anniversary of 'Nostra Aetate' (Declaration on the Relation of the Church with Non-Christian Religions of the Second Vatican Council, 1965), (Vatican, 2015), p14
7 Ian Donald, John McVicar, and Tom Brown, *The investigation of abdominal masses by pulsed ultrasound* (The Lancet, June 7 1958)
8 French Roman Catholic Bishops Statement *End of Life: Yes to the Urgency of Fraternity* (Lourdes, 22 March 2018)
9 Peter Nicholson's testimony *Premier Christian Radio series 'Joy to the World' with Canon John Twisleton* (Premier, Advent 2015)
10 Walter Nigg, *Francis of Assisi* (Mowbrays, 1975), pp16-17
11 Apostles' Creed, Common Worship: Services and Prayers for the Church of England (The Archbishops' Council, 2000), p43
12 John Twisleton, *Why go to Confession?* (Church Union, 1979), pp7-8
13 R.M.French (trans.), *The Way of a Pilgrim*, (SPCK, 1965), p31

14   John Twisleton, *Using the Jesus Prayer*, (BRF, 2014), pp92-95
15   Pope Francis, *Encyclical Letter Laudato Si'* (Vatican Press, 2015) Section 124
16   *Laudato Si'* Section 236
17   Anglican Communion Environmental Network statement from its Chair, Bishop of Canberra, George Browning: https://www.interfaithsustain.com/anglican-views-on-climate-change/
18   *Laudato Si'* Sections 217, 220, 222
19   Austin Farrer, *The End of Man* (SPCK, 1973), p4
20   Thomas Merton, *Seeds of Contemplation* (Dell, 1958), p84
21   Laurens Van der Post, *A Walk with a White Bushman* (Vintage, 1986), p7
22   Clark, *Ecclesiastical History, Life of Queen Elizabeth*, (1675 edition), p94
23   Martin Luther, *Confession Concerning Christ's Supper* (1528), p390
24   Anglican-Roman Catholic International Commission *The Final Report,* (CTS/SPCK 1982), p14
25   Eric Mascall *A Dictionary of Christian Theology* (SCM, 1969), p117
26   Alexander Schmemann quoted in John Twisleton, *Meet Jesus* (BRF, 2011) p65
27   Henri de Lubac, *The Religion of Teilhard de Chardin* (Collins, 1967), pp106, 121, 126, 157, 173
28   E. Kadloubovsky & G.E.H. Palmer (trans.), *Writings from the Philokalia on Prayer of the Heart* (Faber & Faber, 1977)
29   Simon Tugwell, *Did you receive the Spirit?* (Darton, Longman & Todd, 1972)
30   Kilian McDonnell and George T Montague, *Christian Initiation and Baptism in the Holy Spirit* (Liturgical Press, 1991)
31   Pope Francis interviewed in *Francesco* (Documentary directed by Evgeny Afineevsky, 2020)
32   Marriage, *Common Worship: Pastoral Services (The Archbishops' Council, 2000)*, p105
33   The Church of England, *Living in Love and Faith: Christian teaching and learning about identity, sexuality,*

relationships and marriage, (Church House Publishing, 2020)
34   In Christ Alone, *The Stuart Townend Collection* (Kingsway Communications, 2010), pp153-157
35   Eucharistic Prayer III, *The CTS New Sunday Missal* (Catholic Truth Society, 2011), p617
36   Paul Coughlin *Healthy guilt vs. false and harmful guilt* (Focus on the Family, 2008) https://www.focusonthefamily.com/get-help/healthy-guilt-vs-false-and-harmful-guilt/
37   *Quicunque Vult* (Creed of Saint Athanasius) for occasional use at Morning Prayer, *Book of Common Prayer* (1662)
38   Apostles' Creed in Morning and Evening Prayer, *Book of Common Prayer* (1662)
39   CS Lewis, *The Great Divorce,* (Collins, 2012, first edition 1945)
40   Apostles' Creed *Common Worship: Services and Prayers for the Church of England* (The Archbishops' Council, 2000), p141
41   Alan Rusbridger on BBC *Click* 23 January 2021
42   Fyodor Dostoyevsky *Brothers Karamazov in The Collected Works* (Pergamon Media, 2015 Kindle originally published 1880), location 5073
43   HW Baker author of Hymn 515, *Hymns Ancient & Modern Revised* (1972)
44   The Anglican-Roman Catholic International Commission. An Agreed Statement, *Mary Grace and Hope in Christ* (Morehouse, 2005), section 79
45   Walter M Abbott (Ed), *The Documents of Vatican II* (Geoffrey Chapman, 1966), p95
46   John McManners (Editor), *The Oxford Illustrated History of Christianity* (Oxford University Press, 1990), p5-6
47   Pope John Paul II *Apostolic Letter Ordinatio Sacerdotalis of John Paul II to the Bishops of the Catholic Church on reserving priestly ordination to men alone* (1994)
48   House of Bishops *Five Guiding Principles* (2014) https://www.churchofengland.org/sites/default/files/2017-10/the_five_guiding_principles.pdf

49   John Polkinghorne, *Quantum Physics and Theology - an unexpected kinship* (SPCK, 2007) pp32-33

50   Pope John Paul II, *Fides et Ratio* (Encyclical, 1998), pp51-52

51   Eucharistic Preface on the Feast of Christ the King, *Common Worship: Services and Prayers for the Church of England* (The Archbishops' Council, 2000), p327

52   Faith and Order Paper No 111, *Baptism, Eucharist and Ministry* (World Council of Churches, 1982), Preface page ix

53   Tlig.org

54   Brian Leiter, *Why Tolerate Religion?* (Princeton University Press, 2013), pp1-4

55   Kevin O'Donnell, *Inside World Religions: An Illustrated Guide* (Lion, 2006), p13

56   John Twisleton, *Meet Jesus* (Bible Reading Fellowship, 2011), p29

57   Dorothy Sayers, *Creed or Chaos?* (Sophia Institute Press, 1996 reissue), p2

58   Timothy Keller, *The Reason for God* (Hodder & Stoughton, 2008), p25

59   Rowan Williams, *Resurrection: Interpreting the Easter Gospel* (Dartman, Longman & Todd, 2002)

60   John Twisleton, *Pointers to Heaven* (Amazon, 2020) Chapter 9

61   Alexander Schmemann *Journals 1973-1983* (St Vladimir's Seminary, 2000), p71

62   Adele Parks *Just my Luck* (HarperCollins, 2020)

63   Ursula King, *Christ in All Things - exploring Spirituality with Teilhard de Chardin* (Orbis Books, 2016) Kindle location 3337-8

64   John Twisleton *Pointers to Heaven* p9

About the author

John Twisleton is an ideas and people person, theologian and pastor, ministering as a priest in Sussex. He broadcasts on London-based Premier Christian Radio and is well known as an author. His books include Meet Jesus (2011), Using the Jesus Prayer (2014), Experiencing Christ's Love (2017) and Pointers to Heaven (2020).

Books by the author

A History of St Giles Church, Horsted Keynes

Besides being the burial place of former UK Prime Minister Harold Macmillan (1894-1986) and mystic ecumenist Archbishop Robert Leighton (1611-1684) St Giles, Horsted Keynes has association with the history of Sussex back to the 8th century. As 53rd Rector (2009-2017) John Twisleton wrote this illustrated history with the assistance of church members.

Baptism - Some Questions Answered

Illustrated booklet on infant baptism used across the Anglican Communion. It explains the commitments involved in baptising a baby, challenges hypocrisy and attempts to clear up a number of misunderstandings in popular culture about what baptism is all about.

Christianity - Some Questions Answered

This booklet for Christian enquirers attempts dialogue between Christianity and its contemporary critics. A brief inspection of Christian faith clarifies both its unique claims and its universal wisdom so they can be seen and owned more fully.

Confession - Some Questions Answered

Illustrated booklet explaining the value of sacramental confession as an aid to spiritual growth. It commends confession as a helpful discipline serving people as they struggle against sin and guilt and seek to renew church membership.

Empowering Priesthood

This book is an enthusiastic presentation about the gift and calling of the ministerial priesthood. It argues that the choosing and sending of priests is vital to the momentum of mission and that their representation of Christ as priest, prophet and shepherd is given to help build love, consecrate in truth and bring empowerment to the whole priestly body of Christ.

Entering the Prayer of Jesus

Audio CD and booklet prepared by John Twisleton with the Diocese of Chichester and Premier Christian Radio providing spiritual wisdom from across the whole church. Contains audio contributions from Pete Greig (24-7 Prayer), Jane Holloway (Evangelical Alliance), Christopher Jamison (Worth Abbey), Molly Osborne (Lydia Fellowship) and Rowan Williams (Archbishop of Canterbury).

Experiencing Christ's Love

A wake up call to the basic disciplines of worship, prayer, study, service and reflection helpful to loving God, neighbour and self. Against the backdrop of the message of God's love John Twisleton presents a rule of life suited to enter more fully the possibilities of God.

Fifty Walks from Haywards Heath

Sub-titled 'A handbook for seeking space in Mid Sussex' this book celebrates the riches of a town at the heart of Sussex. Through detailed walk routes with schematic illustrations John Twisleton outlines routes from one to thirteen miles with an eye to local history and replenishment of the spirit.

Firmly I Believe

Forty talks suited to Christians or non-Christians explaining the creed, sacraments, commandment and prayer engaging with misunderstandings and objections to faith and its practical expression. Double CD containing 40 easily digested 3 minute talks accompanied by reflective music with full text in the accompanying booklet.

Forty Walks from Ally Pally

John Twisleton explores the byways of Barnet, Camden, Enfield and Haringey with an eye to green spaces, local history and a replenishment of the spirit. The routes, which vary in length between one mile and twenty miles, exploit the public transport network, and are well designed for family outings. The author provides here a practical handbook for seeking space in North London.

Healing - Some Questions Answered

An examination of the healing ministry with suggested ecumenical forms for healing services. The booklet addresses divine intervention, credulity, lay involvement, evil spirits and the healing significance of the e-7—7-ucharist.

Holbrooks History

Illustrated booklet compiled by John Twisleton with members of St Luke's Church, Holbrooks in Coventry about their parish and its church. It describes a multicultural community that has welcomed Irish, West Indian, Eastern European and Indian workers over the last century. The book includes dramatic pictures from the Second World War when the community and its church suffered bomb damage.

Meet Jesus

In a world of competing philosophies, where does Jesus fit in? How far can we trust the Bible and the Church? What difference does Jesus make to our lives and our communities? Is Jesus really the be all and end all? John Twisleton provides a lively and straightforward exploration of these and other questions pointing to how engaging with Jesus expands both mind and heart.

Moorends and its Church

Illustrated booklet telling the tale of the Doncaster suburb of Moorends from the sinking of the pit in 1904 to the 1984-5 mining dispute under the theme of death and resurrection. It includes a community survey of the needs of the elderly, young people and recreational and spiritual needs.

Using the Jesus Prayer

The Jesus Prayer of Eastern Orthodoxy, 'Lord Jesus Christ, Son of God, have mercy on me a sinner' offers a simple yet profound way of deepening spiritual life. John Twisleton gives practical guidance on how to use it outlining the simplification of life it offers.

More at Twisleton.co.uk

JOHN TWISLETON

Printed in Great Britain
by Amazon